Editor
Evan D. Forbes, M.S. Ed.

Editorial Project Manager
Charles Payne, M.A., M.F.A.

Editor in Chief
Sharon Coan, M.S. Ed.

Illustrator
Wendi Wright-Davis

Photo Cover Credit
Images provided by
PhotoDisc ©1994

Art Coordinator
Denice Adorno

Creative Director
Elayne Roberts

Imaging
Evan D. Forbes, M.S. Ed.

Product Manager
Phil Garcia

Publishers
Rachelle Cracchiolo, M.S. Ed.
Mary Dupuy Smith, M.S. Ed.

Hands-On Minds-On Science

Matter

Intermediate

Author
Dr. Kathleen Lewis Thompson

Teacher Created Materials, Inc.
6421 Industry Way
Westminster, CA   92683
www.teachercreated.com
ISBN-1-57690-387-7
©2000 Teacher Created Materials, Inc.
Made in U.S.A.

Table of Contents

Table of Contents *(cont.)*

Introduction

What Is Science?

What is science to young children? Is it something that they know is a part of their world? Is it a textbook in the classroom? Is it a tadpole changing into a frog? Is it a sprouting seed, a rainy day, a boiling pot, a turning wheel, a pretty rock, or a moonlit sky? Is science fun and filled with wonder and meaning? What is science to children?

Science offers you and your eager students opportunities to explore the world around you and make connections between the things you experience. The world becomes your classroom, and you, the teacher, a guide.

Science can, and should, fill children with wonder. It should cause them to be filled with questions and the desire to discover the answers to their questions. And, once they have discovered answers, they should be actively seeking new questions to answer.

The books in this series give you and the students in your classroom the opportunity to learn from the whole of your experiences—the sights, sounds, smells, tastes, and touches, as well as what you read, write about, and do. This whole-science approach allows you to experience and understand your world as you explore science concepts and skills together.

What Is Matter?

Matter is all around us. Everything in our world which takes up space and has weight is "matter." All matter is made up of tiny parts which we cannot see, called molecules, and even tinier parts called atoms. The way these molecules are connected determines if something is a solid, a liquid, or a gas. Heat, cold, and other substances can affect the way matter acts and the form it takes. We have evidence that people have studied matter as long ago as 200 B.C. A basic understanding of what matter is and how it works is essential to both chemistry and physics.

The Scientific Method

The "scientific method" is one of several creative and systematic processes for proving or disproving a given question following an observation. When the scientific method is used in the classroom, a basic set of guiding principles and procedures is followed in order to answer a question. However, real world science is often not as rigid as the scientific method would have us believe.

This systematic method of problem solving will be described in the paragraphs that follow.

1   Make an **OBSERVATION**.

The teacher presents a situation, gives a demonstration, or reads background material that interests students and prompts them to ask questions. Or students can make observations and generate questions on their own as they study a topic.

Example: Have two students try to sit on the same chair at the same time.

2   Select a **QUESTION** to investigate.

In order for students to select a question for a scientific investigation, they will have to consider the materials they have or can get, as well as the resources (books, magazines, people, etc.) actually available to them. You can help them make an inventory of their materials and resources, either individually or as a group.

Tell students that in order to successfully investigate the questions they have selected, they must be very clear about what they are asking. Discuss effective questions with your students. Depending upon their level, simplify the questions or make them more specific.

Example: What will happen if two kinds of matter try to take up the same space at the same time?

3   Make a **PREDICTION** (hypothesis).

Explain to students that a hypothesis is a good guess about what the answer to a question will probably be. But they do not want to make just any arbitrary guess. Encourage students to predict what they think will happen and why. In order to formulate a hypothesis, students may have to gather more information through research.

Have students practice making hypotheses with questions you give them. Tell them to pretend they have already done their research. You want them to write each hypothesis so it follows these rules:

1. It is to the point.
2. It tells what will happen, based on what the question asks.
3. It follows the subject/verb relationship of the question.

Example: I think that one kind of matter will shove the other kind of matter out of the way.

The Scientific Method *(cont.)*

 4 Develop a **PROCEDURE** to test the hypothesis.

The first thing students must do in developing a procedure (the test plan) is to determine the materials they will need.

They must state exactly what needs to be done in step-by-step order. If they do not place their directions in the right order, or if they leave out a step, it becomes difficult for someone else to follow their directions. A scientist never knows when other scientists will want to try the same experiment to see if they end up with the same results!

Example: By placing two kinds of matter in the same place at the same time, we can observe what happens.

 5 Record the **RESULTS** of the investigation in written and picture form.

The results (data collected) of a scientific investigation are usually expressed two ways—in written form and in picture form. Both are summary statements. The written form reports the results with words. The picture form (often a chart or graph) reports the results so the information can be understood at a glance.

Example: The results of the investigation can be recorded on a data-capture sheet.

6 State a **CONCLUSION** that tells what the results of the investigation mean.

The conclusion is a statement which tells the outcome of the investigation. It is drawn after the student has studied the results of the experiment, and it interprets the results in relation to the stated hypothesis. A conclusion statement may read something like either of the following: "The results show that the hypothesis is supported," or "The results show that the hypothesis is not supported." Then restate the hypothesis if it was supported or revise it if it was not supported.

Example: The hypothesis that one kind of matter will shove another kind of matter out of the way if they try to take up the same space was supported (or not supported).

 7 Record **QUESTIONS, OBSERVATIONS**, and **SUGGESTIONS** for future investigations.

Students should be encouraged to reflect on the investigations that they complete. These reflections, like those of professional scientists, may produce questions that will lead to further investigations.

Example: Will heavier matter shove the other matter harder?

Science-Process Skills

Even the youngest students blossom in their ability to make sense out of their world and succeed in scientific investigations when they learn and use the science-process skills. These are the tools that help children think and act like professional scientists.

The first five process skills on the list below are the ones that should be emphasized with young children, but all of the skills will be utilized by anyone who is involved in scientific study.

Observing

It is through the process of observation that all information is acquired. That makes this skill the most fundamental of all the process skills. Children have been making observations all their lives, but they need to be made aware of how they can use their senses and prior knowledge to gain as much information as possible from each experience. Teachers can develop this skill in children by asking questions and making statements that encourage precise observations.

Communicating

Humans have developed the ability to use language and symbols which allow them to communicate not only in the "here and now" but also over time and space as well. The accumulation of knowledge in science, as in other fields, is due to this process skill. Even young children should be able to understand the importance of researching others' communications about science and the importance of communicating their own findings in ways that are understandable and useful to others. The matter journal and the data-capture sheets used in this book are two ways to develop this skill.

Comparing

Once observation skills are heightened, students should begin to notice the relationships among things that they are observing. *Comparing* means noticing similarities and differences. By asking how things are alike and different or which is smaller or larger, teachers will encourage children to develop their comparison skills.

Ordering

Other relationships that students should be encouraged to observe are the linear patterns of seriation (order along a continuum: e.g., rough to smooth, large to small, bright to dim, few to many) and sequence (order along a time line or cycle). By ranking graphs, time lines, cyclical and sequence drawings and by putting many objects in order by a variety of properties, students will grow in their abilities to make precise observations about the order of nature.

Categorizing

When students group or classify objects or events according to logical rationale, they are using the process skill of categorizing. Students begin to use this skill when they group by a single property such as color. As they develop this skill, they will be attending to multiple properties in order to make categorizations; the animal classification system, for example, is one system students can categorize.

Science-Process Skills *(cont.)*

Relating

Relating, which is one of the higher-level process skills, requires student scientists to notice how objects and phenomena interact with one another and the changes caused by these interactions. An obvious example of this is the study of chemical reactions.

Inferring

Not all phenomena are directly observable because they are out of humankind's reach in terms of time, scale, and space. Some scientific knowledge must be logically inferred based on the data that is available. Much of the work of paleontologists, astronomers, and those studying the structure of matter is done by inference.

Applying

Even very young, budding scientists should begin to understand that people have used scientific knowledge in practical ways to change and improve the way we live. It is at this application level that science becomes meaningful for many students.

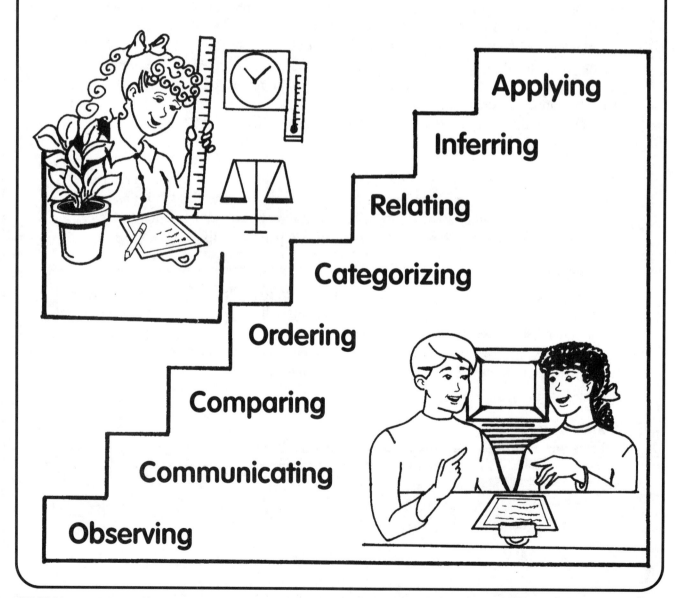

Organizing Your Unit

Designing a Science Lesson

In addition to the lessons presented in this unit, you will want to add lessons of your own, lessons that reflect the unique environment in which you live, as well as the interests of your students. When designing new lessons or revising old ones, try to include the following elements in your planning:

Question

Pose a question to your students that will guide them in the direction of the experiment you wish to perform. Encourage all answers, but you want to lead the students towards the experiment you are going to be doing. Remember, there must be an observation before there can be a question. (Refer to The Scientific Method, pages 5–6.)

Setting the Stage

Prepare your students for the lesson. Brainstorm to find out what students already know. Have children review books to discover what is already known about the subject. Invite them to share what they have learned.

Materials Needed for Each Group or Individual

List the materials each group or individual will need for the investigation. Include a data-capture sheet when appropriate.

Procedure

Make sure students know the steps to take to complete the activity. Whenever possible, ask them to determine the procedure. Make use of assigned roles in group work. Create (or have your students create) a data-capture sheet. Ask yourself, "How will my students record and report what they have discovered? Will they tally, measure, draw, or make a checklist? Will they make a graph? Will they need to preserve specimens?" Let students record results orally, using a videotape or audiotape recorder. For written recording, encourage students to use a variety of paper supplies such as poster board or index cards. It is also important for students to keep journals of their investigation activities. Journals can be made of lined and unlined paper. Students can design their own covers. The pages can be stapled or be put together with paper fasteners or spiral binding.

Extensions

Continue the success of the lesson. Consider which related skills or information you can tie into the lesson, like math, language arts skills, or something being learned in social studies. Make curriculum connections frequently and involve the students in making these connections. Extend the activity, whenever possible, to home investigations.

Closure

Encourage students to think about what they have learned and how the information connects to their own lives. Prepare matter journals using the directions on page 86. Provide an ample supply of blank and lined pages for students to use as they complete the closure activities. Allow time for students to record their thoughts and pictures in their journals.

Organizing Your Unit *(cont.)*

Structuring Student Groups for Scientific Investigations

Using cooperative learning strategies in conjunction with hands-on and discovery learning methods will benefit all the students taking part in the investigation.

Cooperative Learning Strategies

1. In cooperative learning, all group members need to work together to accomplish the task.

2. Cooperative learning groups should be heterogeneous.

3. Cooperative learning activities need to be designed so that each student contributes to the group and individual group members can be assessed on their performance.

4. Cooperative learning teams need to know the social as well as the academic objectives of a lesson.

Cooperative Learning Groups

Groups can be determined many ways for the scientific investigations in your class. Here is one way of forming groups that has proven to be successful in intermediate classrooms.

*   **The Team Leader**—scientist in charge of reading directions and setting up equipment.

*   **Lab Technician**—scientist in charge of carrying out directions (can be more than one student).

*   **The Stenographer**—scientist in charge of recording all of the information.

*   **The Transcriber**—scientist who translates notes and communicates findings.

If the groups remain the same for more than one investigation, require each group to vary the people chosen for each job. All group members should get a chance to try each job at least once.

Using Centers for Scientific Investigations

Set up stations for each investigation. To accommodate several groups at a time, stations may be duplicated for the same investigation. Each station should contain directions for the activity, all necessary materials (or a list of materials for investigators to gather), a list of words (a word bank) which students may need for writing and speaking about the experience, and any data-capture sheets or needed materials for recording and reporting data and findings.

Just the Facts

Matter is all around us. Everything which takes up space and has weight is matter. There are three kinds of matter: solids, liquids, gases. All matter is made up of tiny parts called molecules. The word molecules comes from a Latin word meaning "little mass."

Molecules

Molecules are tiny particles that can't be seen without a microscope. Molecules are the smallest part of a solid, liquid or gas which can exist and still retain the characteristics of the solid, liquid, or gas. For instance, if you separate a puddle of water into small parts, you will still have water, regardless of how small the parts are. An Italian chemist, Count Amedeo Avogadro (1776–1856) calculated that there are 602,000,000,000,000,000,000,000 molecules in 18 grams of water, which is about the size of a thimble!

Molecules are made up of smaller parts called atoms. Each water molecule is made up of two atoms of hydrogen and one atom of oxygen. If you separate the atoms of water, you would have hydrogen and oxygen, two different gases.

The space between molecules determines if matter is a liquid, a solid, or a gas. All matter has forces or bonds between its molecules, which also vary according to the form, or state, of matter. According to the kinetic theory, molecules are always moving. Regardless of the differences in the space between the molecules, the strength of the bonds between molecules, or the movement of the molecules, all matter has two characteristics in common: 1) matter takes up space 2) matter has weight or mass.

Solids

Solids are matter which have a fixed shape and volume. The molecules are close together and the bonds between them are rigid. Their movement is more of a vibration, since they cannot move freely.

Solids can sit by themselves, have a shape of their own, and can be seen and felt. Other matter cannot pass easily through solids because there is little space between its molecules and the bonds between molecules are strong. Solids have weight and take up space.

Liquids

Liquids are matter which have definite volume, but no definite shape. The molecules are spaced apart and the bonds between them are loose. The loose bonds allow free movement of the molecules.

Just the Facts *(cont.)*

Liquids *(cont.)*

Liquids can be seen and felt and are wet to the touch. They have no definite shape and cannot sit by themselves, but rather take the shape of the container in which they are held. Liquids can be poured, and other matter can pass easily through them because there is space between the molecules and the bonds are looser than those of solids and can be easily broken. Liquids have weight and take up space.

Gases

Gases are matter which have no definite volume or shape. The molecules are widely spaced and the bonds between are them are very loose. The loose bonds allow free movement of the molecules.

Gases cannot be seen or felt, but they can be poured because they are fluids. They cannot sit by themselves or have a shape of their own. Other matter can pass easily through gases because the molecules are widely spaced and the bonds are very loose. Gases have weight and take up space.

Discovering the Definition of Matter—Solid, Liquid, Gas

Question

What two characteristics do all types of matter have?

Setting the Stage

- Show the students a book, a soda, and blow air in front of you. Tell them that all three of these things are called "Matter." The book is a "solid," the soda (pour the soda so they see you're talking about the liquid, rather than the can) is a "liquid," and your breath is a "gas."
- Today the class will carefully examine solids, liquids, and gases in order to learn characteristics about them, and to discover what two things are the same about all three kinds of matter. The word "matter" is defined by those two things that are the same.

Materials Needed for Each Group

- water in small container (amount is not important)
- larger empty container
- a set of Matter Observation sheets on colored paper (pink=solid, green=gas, blue=liquid)
- a solid object (vary them among teams so that no team has the same object)
- a ruler
- three 4" (10 cm) pieces of string
- two balloons

Procedure (*Student Instructions*)

1. Examine each solid object and complete your Solid Observation sheet.
2. Examine the water, not the container. Before you begin writing your observations, pour the water into the other container, and watch what happens to the shape of the water, then complete your Liquid Observation sheet.
3. Examine your breath, a gas. Blow air, or gas, out of your body and complete all of the Gas Observation sheet except for "Does it have weight?." For that question:

    -Blow up one balloon.
    -Tie it with a string to the 1" (2.5 cm) mark on the ruler.
    -Tie the empty balloon to the 11" (27.5 cm) mark on the ruler.
    -Tie the other piece of string to the 6" (15 cm) mark on the ruler.
    -Hold the ruler by the string on the 6" (15 cm) mark and observe the other balloons to see which is heavier. (If students have difficulty seeing which is heavier, draw a straight line on the board and have students hold the ruler with balloons in front of it, so they can see that one side is slightly heavier).
    -Lay out all three Matter Observation sheets and find what two things are the same for all kinds of matter. (The teacher should point out that the only two things which are the same for all kinds of matter have weight and take up space.) Provide the definition of matter, which is anything that takes up space and has weight.

Discovering the Definition of Matter—Solid, Liquid, Gas *(cont.)*

Extensions:

- Have students find examples of "liquids," "solids," and "gases" at home.
- Color water and pour it into clear containers of different shapes to better illustrate the fact that liquids take the shape of the object containing them.
- Have students write riddles about things around them, using the characteristics of each type of matter.

Closure

- In their science journals, have students title one page "Matter." Divide the page into three sections labeled "Solid," "Liquid," and "Gas," and draw an example for each.
- Have students title another page "Principles of Matter" and list the two they learned today. (1. All matter has weight. 2. All matter takes up space.)

The Big Why

This activity gives students an opportunity to explore characteristics of types of matter and to learn the definition of matter through self-discovery.

Discovering the Definition of Matter—Solid, Liquid, Gas *(cont.)*

SOLID

_____
Team Name

Does it sit by itself? _____

Does it have a shape of its own? _____

Can you see it? _____

Can you feel it? _____

Does it have weight? _____

Does it flow? _____

Can you pour it? _____

Does it feel wet? _____

Does it take up space? _____

Can a solid pass through it easily? _____

Discovering the Definition of Matter—Solid, Liquid, Gas *(cont.)*

Liquid

_____
Team Name

Does it sit by itself?   _____

Does it have a shape of its own?   _____

Can you see it?   _____

Can you feel it?   _____

Does it have weight?   _____

Does it flow?   _____

Can you pour it?   _____

Does it feel wet?   _____

Does it take up space?   _____

Can a solid pass through it easily?   _____

Discovering the Definition of Matter—Solid, Liquid, Gas *(cont.)*

Gas

_____
Team Name

Does it sit by itself?   _____

Does it have a shape of its own?   _____

Can you see it?   _____

Can you feel it?   _____

Does it have weight?   _____

Does it flow?   _____

Can you pour it?   _____

Does it feel wet?   _____

Does it take up space?   _____

Can a solid pass through it easily?   _____

A Closer Look at Liquids

Question

Are all liquids the same?

Setting the Stage

- Review the observations of matter, especially the characteristics of liquids.
- Have students ascertain which characteristic(s) of liquids are distinct and true only for liquids. You might blindfold a student and have him/her feel a solid and a liquid and identify them by type of matter. Ask how he/she could so easily identify the liquid.
- Tell students that today they are going to further examine liquids to see if they are all the same. They will use their eyes, noses, hands, and brains in this observation.
- Write this Word Bank of adjectives on the board as a springboard for descriptions: clear, sticky, wet, sweet, greasy, yellow, sharp, heavy, slowly, and quickly.

Materials Needed for Each Group

- four clear plastic cups, each containing 1/4 cup (62.5 mL) of the following: water, honey or syrup, vinegar, cooking oil
- four plastic baggies
- a spring scale
- newspapers covering table/desks
- data-capture sheet (page 20)

Procedure (*Student Directions*)

1. Feel each liquid and record what you feel on your data-capture sheet.
2. Smell each liquid and record what you smell on your data-capture sheet.
3. Look at the liquids and record their color on your data-capture sheet.
4. Pour one liquid from the cup into the plastic baggie. Observe how it pours and record what you see on your data-capture sheet.
5. Weigh the liquid in its plastic baggie on the spring scale and record the weight on the data-capture sheet.
6. Pour a little of the liquid on your newspaper to see if it can sit by itself or if it spreads all over the newspaper.
7. Repeat the six steps with your other liquids.
8. Answer the questions at the bottom of your data-capture sheet.

Extensions

- Have students take blank copies of the data-capture sheet home and make observations of other liquids, except for the weighing observation.
- Have students construct graphs comparing the weight of the same amount of varying liquids (e.g., motor oil, water, honey, soda, etc.).
- Measure liquids, then pour them into different sized containers. Although they might appear to be "bigger" in some containers, remeasurement will prove that the amount of liquid has not changed, just its shape.

A Closer Look at Liquids *(cont.)*

Closure

Discuss the observations. Ascertain which things the student teams found to be similar about the liquids and which they found to be different. Have students make notes about these findings in their science journal.

The Big Why

Students make close observations of liquids in order to ascertain their similarities and differences.

A Closer Look at Liquids *(cont.)*

Team Name _____

Date _____

Liquids	How does it feel?	How does it smell?	What color is it?	How does it pour?	How many grams does it weigh?	Can it sit by itself?
Water						
Honey						
Vinegar						
Cooking Oil						

Was there anything the same about all the liquids? If so, what? _____

Was there anything different about some of the liquids? If so, What? _____

A Closer Look at Solids

Question

Are all solids the same?

Setting the Stage

- Review what students know about matter - the 3 types and their characteristics, as well as the detailed observation of liquids.
- Show students a piece of paper and a book. Ask them what form of matter these objects are. Allow several students in the class to feel them and pick them up to compare their weight.
- Ask them if the objects are alike in any way and if they can identify which type of matter these objects are. If they have trouble, ask them if the objects can be seen (therefore they are not gases), if they are wet (therefore they are not liquids), etc., leading them to the fact that although these two objects seem very different, they are both solids.
- Tell students that today they will make close observations of some solids in order to see what things are the same and different about solids. They will complete a data-capture sheet much like the one on liquids, and will need their eyes, noses, ears, and brains.
- Write this Word Bank of adjectives on the board as a springboard for descriptions: heavy, light, hard, soft, rough, smooth, pliable, rubbery, and earthy.

Materials Needed for Each Group

- a spring scale
- four plastic sandwich bags
- a ruler
- a bowl

*All of the following materials should be about the same size.

- several cotton balls formed to about the size of a jacks ball
- a small rubber ball about the size of a jacks ball
- a wad of clay about the size of a jacks ball
- a wad of paper about the size of a jacks ball
- data-capture sheet (page 23)

Procedure (*Student Directions*)

1. Feel each solid and record what you feel on your data-capture sheet.
2. Smell each solid and record what you smell on your data-capture sheet.
3. Look at the solids and record their color on your data-capture sheet.
4. Put each solid in the bowl. Do they keep their own shape as they sit in the bowl or do they take the shape of the bowl?
5. Weigh the solid in its plastic baggie on the spring scale and record the weight on the data-capture sheet.
6. Put the solid on the table to see if it can sit by itself.
7. Repeat the six steps with your other solids.
8. Answer the questions at the bottom of your data-capture sheet.

A Closer Look at Solids *(cont.)*

Extensions

- Give students Venn diagrams and have them compare and contrast liquids and solids.
- Using Venn diagrams, compare and contrast the solids which students examined.
- Compare the weight of wet and dry objects. Use both absorbent and nonabsorbent materials. Ask students why the wet absorbent objects weigh more (they contain two kinds of matter).

Closure

Discuss the observations. Ascertain which things the student teams found to be similar about the solids and which they found to be different. Have students make notes about these findings in their science journal.

The Big Why

Students make close observations of solids in order to ascertain their similarities and differences.

A Closer Look at Solids *(cont.)*

Team Name _____

Date _____

Solids	How does it feel?	How does it smell?	What color is it?	Does it have its own shape?	How many grams does it weigh?	Can it sit by itself?
Cotton Ball						
Rubber Ball						
Clay Ball						
Paper Ball						

Was there anything the same about all the solids? If so, what? _____

Was there anything different about some of the solids? If so, What? _____

Molecules

Question

Why isn't all matter the same?

Setting the Stage

- Tell them that all matter is made up of tiny little pieces called molecules, too small for our eyes to see. Show them a tinker toy model of molecules (connect balls by small straight pieces). Tell them that the distance that these molecules stay from each other determines if something will be a solid, liquid, or gas. The bonds, or small pieces which hold them together, are different also.

- Tell them that in a solid, the molecules are very close together and their bonds are very tight. It is hard for anything else to get through the molecules and their bonds. Have a student team come up and demonstrate, forming a "huddle." Demonstrate that it is difficult to get through the solid because its molecules are so close together and its bonds are so tight.

- Tell them that in a liquid, the molecules are spread out a little, and the bonds are a little looser. Ask the student molecule team to demonstrate by moving arms' length apart, holding hands. Demonstrate that you now can get through them by weaving between their spaces/bonds.

- Tell them that in a gas, the molecules are spread really far apart (have the team demonstrate by moving far apart). Because they are so far apart, their bonds are also very light. Hand the gas molecules a ball of string and thread it around to all the team members. Demonstrate that it is very easy to get through these molecules and their bonds because they are so far apart and the bonds spread thinly. It is also difficult to see all of these molecules at one time.

- Today they will be make some observations to see which kinds of matter can get through the molecules and bonds in other kinds of matter. Demonstrate with the first item on the data-capture sheet, having them drop a spoonful of water in the middle of a desk, then feeling underneath to see if the liquid could pass through the solid. After they observe that it cannot get through, discuss the last column on the data-capture sheet, "Why could/couldn't the other matter pass through?." They might mention that the molecules were too close together and/or the bonds between the molecules were too tight.

Materials Needed for Each Group

- a bowl of water
- a book
- a small rock
- a spoon
- a straw
- a data-capture sheet (page 26)

Procedure *(Student Instructions)*

1. Read your data-capture sheet and follow the directions in column 1.

2. Record your observation about whether the water (a liquid) could get through the desk (a solid) in column 2.

3. Explain what you saw in column 3. Be certain to talk about molecules and/or their bonds in your answer. Think about how far apart or close together the molecules must have been, as well as how tight or loose their bonds must have been to explain what you saw in your observation.

Molecules *(cont.)*

Extension

Have students make models of the molecules in liquids, solids, and gases by gluing Styrofoam "peanuts" inside plastic baggies.

Closure

- In their science journals, have students divide a page into three sections, "solid," "liquid," and "gas," then draw the molecules in each.
- Have students turn to the "Principles of Matter" page in their journal and enter, "The space and bonds between molecules decides if something is a solid, liquid, or gas."

The Big Why

Students try to pass one type of matter through another in order to determine the configuration and bonds of molecules in different states of matter.

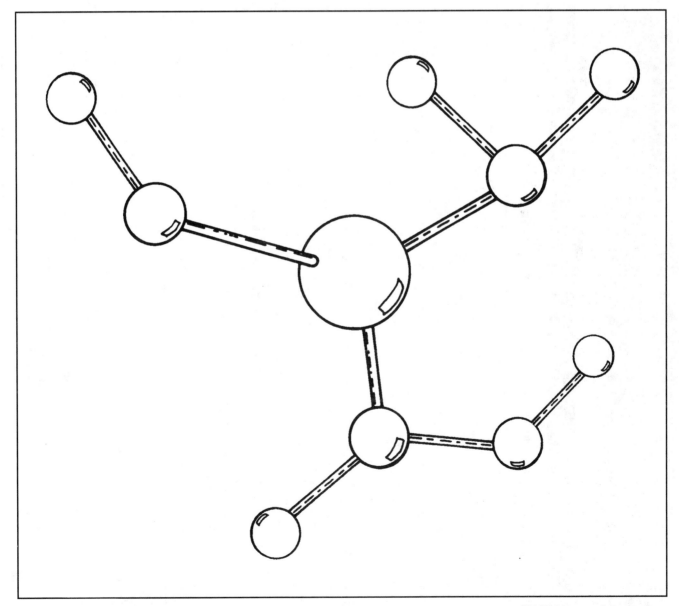

Molecules *(cont.)*

Team Name _____   Date _____

Kind of Matter	Did the matter get through?	Why could/couldn't the other matter get through?
A liquid getting through a solid * Pour a spoonful of water (liquid) on the middle of the desk (solid). Feel under the desk to see if the liquid got through.	Yes ___ No ___	
A liquid getting through a gas * Blow breath (gas) over a bowl of water. Try to pour water through the breath. Look and feel to see if it got through.	Yes ___ No ___	
A solid getting through a liquid * Try to put a rock (solid) into a bowl of water (liquid). Look to see if it got through.	Yes ___ No ___	
A solid getting through a gas * Blow breath (gas) out of your body. Try to pass a book (solid) through. Look to see if it got through.	Yes ___ No ___	
A gas getting through a solid * Blow breath (gas) on the middle of the desk (solid). Feel underneath to see if the gas got through.	Yes ___ No ___	
A gas getting through a liquid * Blow breath (gas) through a straw into a bowl of water (liquid). Look to see if it got through.	Yes ___ No ___	

It's a Matter of Space

Question

What will happen if two kinds of matter try to take up the same space at the same time?

Setting the Stage

- Have two students come to the front of the room and play musical chairs with one chair. Ask the class what happened when they both tried to take up the same space at the same time.

- Have a team come up to form a liquid molecule shape (standing slightly apart, holding hands). Have another team come up and huddle like a solid molecule shape. Ask them to enter the "liquid" molecule team. The liquid molecules will have to spread apart to let them in.

- Remind students that one of the two things which are true for all kinds of matter is that matter takes up space. They just saw that when two students try to take up the same space at the same time, one of them has to leave.

- Today they will do an experiment in which they investigate what happens when two kinds of matter try to take up the same space at the same time. In this experiment, they will need to carefully measure, using both a measuring cup and a ruler.

- Review measuring procedures, pointing out that when using a measuring cup they must first be certain that they are using the correct measuring cup, then, that the cup is filled to the top. If they spill what is in the cup they will need to remeasure.

- Demonstrate setting the #1 cm end of a ruler on the table next to a cup and reading the measurement next to a line on the cup.

- Discuss and demonstrate that to determine how much space matter took up, they will need to first measure the water in a cup before any matter is added, then measure the water after the matter is added. They will then need to subtract the first measurement from the second in order to see how much space was taken up.

Materials Needed for Each Group

- three clear plastic cups
- 3/4 cup (187.5 mL) of water
- 3/4 cup (187.5 mL) of juice
- 3/4 cup (187.5 mL) of beans
- a straw
- one set of measuring cups
- a ruler
- one experiment sheet
- data-capture sheet

Procedure

1. Discuss the question. Thinking about what you have observed around you and learned in class, make a team hypothesis. Write it on your experiment sheet.

2. Follow the procedure steps on your experiment sheet. Be certain to check off each step as you do it. Complete your data-capture sheet as you work.

It's a Matter of Space *(cont.)*

Procedure *(cont.)*

3. Write the results of your experiment, telling what you actually saw happening. Talk about the materials you used in the experiment.

4. Discuss the conclusion. Remember that you are trying to answer the experiment question. Be sure that you have a because statement in the conclusion, and talk about the molecules.

Extensions

- Have students do a Writing to Inform exercise. Ask them to explain to a student in another class what they did in this experiment, using sequence words, and tell what they discovered.

- Put a hole in the bottom of a large empty juice can. Place the can upside down in a bucket of water, having students place their hands near the hole. As water enters the can, they will feel air rushing out of the can. As the water enters the space inside the can, it pushes the air which was there out, since they both cannot take up the same space at the same time.

- Try two short experiments to show that ice takes up more space than water: 1) Fill a bottle to the top with water and make a loose fitting cap out of aluminum foil. Put the bottle in the freezer until the contents are frozen. The ice will expand, pushing the top off. The molecules in ice have a different configuration than the molecules in water. 2) Float an ice cube in a glass of water that is almost full. Have students watch what happens to the water line as the ice melts.

Closure

- Discuss the experiment hypotheses, results, and conclusions. Examine the team charts to make certain that all the teams got the same measurements for the first step of each part of the experiment. Everyone should have the same cm measurement for 1/2 cup (125 mL) of water, every time. The experiment results will be affected if the measurements weren't properly taken.

- Discuss the fact that the solids and liquids were carefully measured, but there was no way to carefully measure gas, so that the experiment cannot fully compare a gas with the liquid and solid.

- Have students make a science journal entry: "Two kinds of matter cannot stay in the same space at the same time."

The Big Why

Students conduct an experiment in which they prove that two kinds of matter cannot take up the same space at the same time.

It's a Matter of Space *(cont.)*

Science Experiment Form

Team Name_____ Date_____

Question (What do I want to find out?)

What will happen if two kinds of matter try to take up the same space at the same time?

Hypothesis (What do I think or guess will happen?)

_____

_____

Procedures (What are the steps to find out?)

1. Adding a solid to a liquid

a. Use your measuring cups to put 1/4 cup of water into a clear plastic cup.

b. Use your marker to draw a line on the cup which shows how high the water is in the cup now. Do not draw a line which goes up and down. Draw a line straight across the cup. Record the measurement on the data-capture sheet.

c. Use your measuring cups to put 1/4 cup of beans in the cup.

d. Put a new mark on the cup to show how high the water is in the cup now.

e. Measure the mark and record it on your data-capture sheet.

f. Subtract the first mark from the second mark to see how much space the solid took up and record it on your data-capture sheet.

2. Adding a gas to a liquid

a. Put 1/4 cup (62.5 mL) water in another plastic cup and draw a line to show how high the water is.

b. Use your ruler to measure the line and record the measurement on your data-capture sheet.

c. Put your straw in the water and blow some gas into it while another team member puts a mark on the cup to show how high the water in the cup went when you blew gas into it.

d. Measure the mark and record it on your data-capture sheet.

e. Subtract the first mark from the gas mark to see how much space the gas took up and record it on your data-capture sheet.

It's a **Matter of Space** *(cont.)*

Science Experiment Form *(cont.)*

3. Adding a liquid to a liquid

a. Put 1/4 cup (62.5 mL) water in another plastic cup and draw a line to show how high the water is.

b. Measure the line. Record the measurement on your data-capture sheet.

c. Use your measuring cups to put 1/4 cup (62.5 mL) of juice in the cup of water.

d. Put a mark on the cup to show how high the water in the cup went when you put another liquid into it.

e. Measure the mark and record it on your data-capture sheet.

f. Subtract the first mark from the second mark to see how much space the other liquid took up and record it on your data-capture sheet.

Results (What did I see actually happen?)

1. Adding a solid to a liquid _____

_____

2. Adding a gas to a liquid _____

_____

3. Adding a liquid to a liquid_____

_____

Conclusion (What is the answer to the question?)

_____

_____

_____

_____

_____

It's a Matter of Space *(cont.)*

What will happen if two kinds of matter try to take up the same space at the same time?

Team Name _____

Date _____

Beginning Water Measurement	Water Measurement After Matter Is Added	Amount of Space the Matter Took Up
Part 1: The water was ___ cm high before any matter was added.	The water was ___ cm high after the beans were added.	The beans took up ___ cm of space in the water.
Part 2: The water was ___ cm high before any matter was added.	The water was ___ cm high after the gas was added.	The gas took up ___ cm of space in the water.
Part 3: The water was ___ cm high before any matter was added.	The water was ___ cm high after the juice was added.	The juice took up ___ cm of space in the water.

Air and Space

Question

Does air take up space?

Setting the Stage

- Review what happened in the experiment yesterday.
- Tell students that today they will be learning about "air." Ask them what they know about "air." Ask them if "air" is matter.
- If they did not suggest it, offer the information that "air," which is all around us, consists of invisible gases. Thus "air" is matter, in the form of a gas. One of the gases is called "oxygen" and another is called "carbon dioxide." The plants, animals, and people on earth cannot live without the air. We can live for a few days without food, but we can't live more than five minutes without air.
- Tell them that some of the air around us enters our bodies. When you blow your air, or gases, from your body, into a balloon, you can see proof that those gases exist in your body, even though you can't see them. Blow up a balloon for demonstration.
- Tell students that the question they will be investigating today is, "Does air take up space?." In the investigation today, they will be using experiment sheets and observation sequence charts. The person on the team chosen as Observation Artist has the job of drawing pictures of each step in the experiment, as the experiment takes place. This person must be observant and stay on task in order to draw quickly and accurately.

Materials Needed for Each Group

- newspapers
- large, deep, clear container filled 3/4 full of water
- one small, clear cup or glass
- one paper towel
- Science Experiment Form (page 34)
- Observation Chart (page 35)

Procedure

1. Discuss the question. Thinking about what you have observed around you and learned in class, make a team hypothesis. Write it on your experiment sheet.
2. Follow the procedure steps on your experiment sheet. Be certain to check off each step as you do it. Complete your observation sequence sheet as you work.
3. Write the results of your experiment, telling what you actually saw happening. Talk about the materials you used in the experiment.
4. Discuss the conclusion. Remember that you are trying to answer the experiment question. Be sure that you have a because statement in the conclusion, and talk about the molecules.

Air and Space *(cont.)*

Extensions

- Float a cork in a bowl of water. Turn a clear, plastic glass upside down and push it down into the water over the cork. The cork will sink because the air inside the glass pushed the water out of the glass' "space." Cork can float on water, but not on air. When air filled the inside of the glass, rather than water, the cork sank.

- Have students write a story from the viewpoint of the paper towel in their experiment. It might begin with something like: "It was just another day. I was hanging around on my roll when suddenly a little boy pulled me off and crumpled me up into a ball. Ouch!" Be certain that students write about "air" in their story.

Closure

Discuss what they observed in the experiment, asking them why the towel didn't get wet. Be certain that they all understand that air was taking up space in the little cup. Remind them that two kinds of matter cannot stay in the same place at the same time, as they saw yesterday. In this instance, the air was taking up space in the cup. Because it was taking up space, the water couldn't get in.

The Big Why

Students conduct an experiment in which they observe that air takes up space.

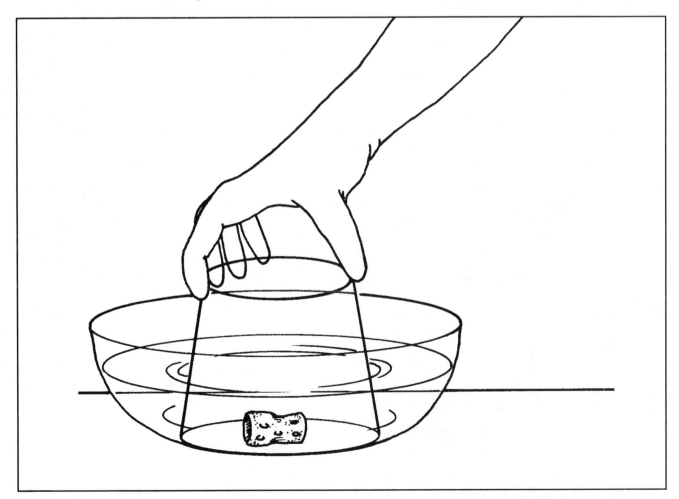

Air and Space *(cont.)*

Science Experiment Form

Team Name_____ Date_____

Question (What do I want to find out?)

Does air take up space?

Hypothesis (What do I think or guess will happen?)

_____

_____

Procedures (What are the steps to find out?)

1. Push the towel into the little glass firmly so that it stays in the glass when you turn it upside down.
2. Turn the cup upside down.
3. Holding the cup by the top, push it straight down into the water. Hold it there until you count to 30.
4. Lift the cup straight up out of the water.
5. Pull the towel out and examine it.

Results (What did I see actually happen?)

_____

_____

_____

Conclusion (What is the answer to the question?)

_____

_____

_____

_____

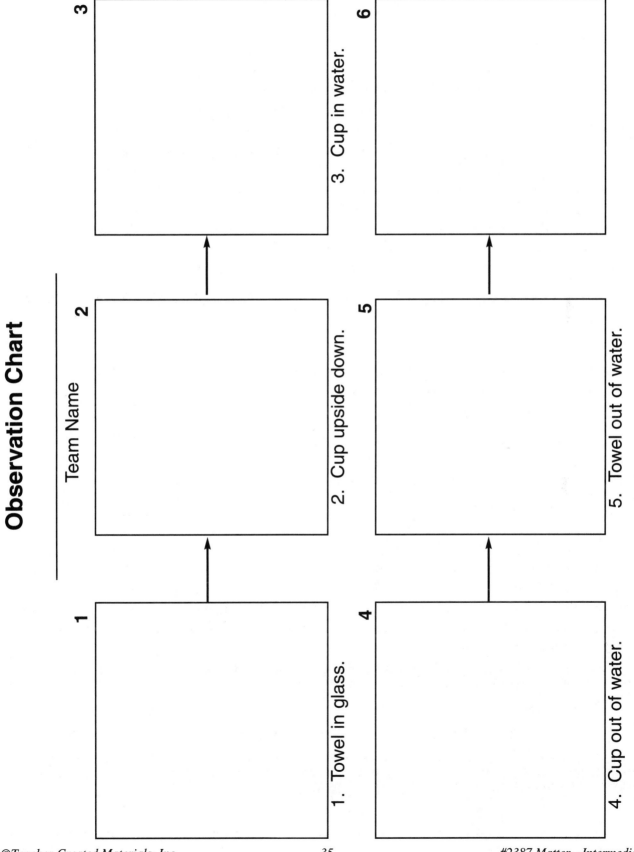

Air and Space *(cont.)*

Observation Chart

Team Name

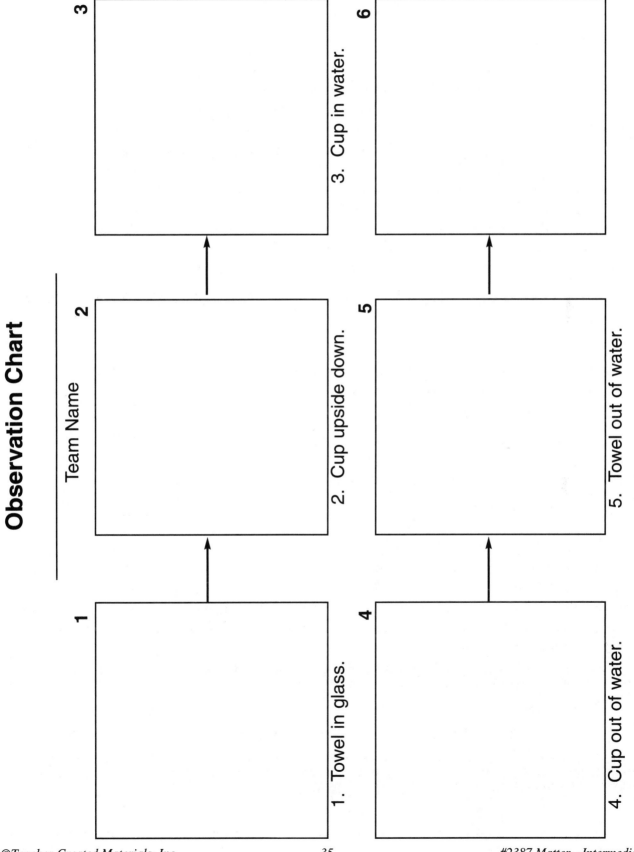

1. Towel in glass.

2. Cup upside down.

3. Cup in water.

4. Cup out of water.

5. Towel out of water.

Weight and Space

Question

Is there a relationship between the weight of a floating object and the space it takes up?

Setting the Stage

- Review the two properties of matter (they take up space and have weight).
- Discuss the observation in which different kinds of liquids and solids were weighed, as well as the experiment in which they observed that all objects take up space.
- Tell students that today they will again be weighing matter, but they will need to do some good thinking. Today they will be weighing different solids, then placing them in water. They will measure the water which the solid objects pushes out of the way, and see if the weight of the object had any relationship to the amount of water it pushed out of the way.
- Review use/reading of the spring scale, as well as the lines on the measuring cup. Be certain to point out that today they will need to read the "oz" side of the scale, rather than the gram side, because they will be comparing the ounces on the spring scale with the ounces in the measuring cup.

Materials Needed for Each Group

- plastic baggie
- a set of measuring cups
- a clear 2 cup (500 mL) measuring cup, with ounces marked on the side
- a spring scale, with ounce readings
- newspapers
- about two cups (500 mL) of water
- one small orange, one lemon, one small onion
- experiment sheet (page 38)
- data-capture sheet (page 39)

Procedure

1. Discuss the question. Thinking about what you have observed around you and learned in class, make a team hypothesis. Write it on your experiment sheet.
2. Follow the procedure steps on your experiment sheet. Be certain to check off each step as you do it. Be certain to measure carefully, recording your measurements on your data-capture sheet as you work.
3. Write the results of your experiment, telling what you actually saw happening. Talk about the materials you used in the experiment.
4. Discuss the conclusion. Remember that you are trying to answer the experiment question. Be sure that you have a because statement in the conclusion, and talk about the molecules.

Weight and Space *(cont.)*

Extensions

- Try the experiment with sinking objects, to see if Archimedes' Principle holds true. For instance, flatten a small piece of clay and float it in the water, checking the amount of water it displaces. Then ball the clay up and place it in the water. It will sink. Measure the amount of water of it displaces.
- Research Archimedes and his other discoveries.

Closure

- Discuss team results. Ask what factors may have affected team findings (mismeasurement, misreading, faulty functioning of spring scale).
- Tell them that a man named Archimedes who lived in 200 B.C. did many investigations like the one the class did today. Since he did the same investigation so many times, he could make sure that what he found was correct, and that he had made no errors in measuring. He found that when a floating object is placed in water, the amount of water it pushes aside is exactly equal to what that object weighs. So this is what they should have found in their experiment today. If they didn't, they must have made some errors in measuring or reading measurements.
- Make a science journal entry about what was learned in the investigation today: "When a floating object is placed in water, the amount of water it pushes aside is exactly equal to the weight of the object."

The Big Why

Students conduct an experiment in which they discover that the weight of a floating object placed in water is exactly equal to the amount of water it displaces.

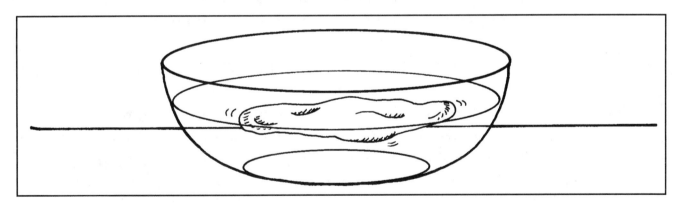

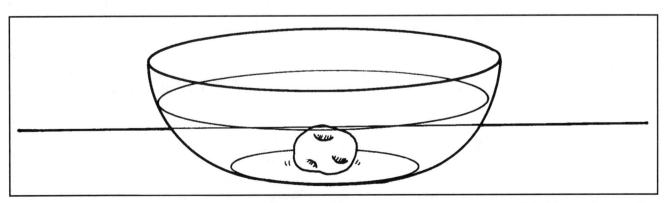

Weight and Space *(cont.)*

Science Experiment Form

Team Name_____ Date_____

Question (What do I want to find out?)

Is there a relationship between the weight of a floating object and the space it takes up?

Hypothesis (What do I think or guess will happen?)

_____

_____

Procedures (What are the steps to find out?)

1. Put your orange in the plastic baggie.
2. Put the hook of the spring scale through the top of the baggie to see how many ounces the orange weighs.
3. Record the weight of the orange on your data-capture sheet. Take the orange out of the baggie and set it aside.
4. Pour 1 cup (250 mL) of water into your large glass measuring cup.
5. On your data-capture sheet, record the "ounces" of the water in the measuring cup.
6. Put the orange carefully in the measuring cup, making certain not to splash the water.
7. Read the new water measurement of the measuring cup and record the ounces on your data-capture sheet.
8. Subtract the "water measurement before" from the "water measurement after" and write that figure in the last column of your data-capture sheet.
9. Take the orange out and repeat steps 1–7 with your other objects. Make certain that you have 1 cup (250 mL) of water in your glass measuring cup before you begin again.

Results (What did I see actually happen?)

_____

Conclusion (What is the answer to the question?)

_____

Weight and Space *(cont.)*

Does the weight of a floating object have a relationship to the space it takes up?

Team Name _____

Date _____

Weight of Solid	Water Measurement Before Object Is Put In	Water Measurement After Object Is Put In	Difference in Water Measurement
Orange ____ ounces	____ ounces	____ ounces	____ ounces
Lemon ____ ounces	____ ounces	____ ounces	____ ounces
Onion ____ ounces	____ ounces	____ ounces	____ ounces

Do you see any relationship between the weight of the solid (Column 1) and the differences you got when you subtracted the "before water measurement" from the "after water measurement" (Column 4)?

What is the relationship? _____

_____

_____

Just the Facts

According to the kinetic theory, molecules are always moving. The constant movement of molecules is called the Brownian movement, for the Scottish scientist, Dr. Robert Brown (1773–1858), who first studied it. The tight bonds of the molecules in a solid only allow the molecules to vibrate back and forth, while the loose bonds of liquids and gasses allow their molecules to move freely. They move like bumper cars, bumping into each other, bouncing away, then back again. The movement of molecules is affected by heat and cold.

Temperature and the Speed of Molecules

The rate at which molecules move depends on the degree of heat to which the molecules are exposed. If matter is exposed to cold, the movement of the molecules are slow or sluggish, but when molecules are exposed to heat, the molecular movement speeds up. The speed of a substance's molecules is a measure of how hot or cold the substance is.

For instance, when two hot liquids are combined, their molecules will very quickly spread out because the molecules are smashing hard together. Thus, the molecules of the two liquids will quickly mix together. If the molecules are cold, the molecules will move slowly and it will take longer for them to mix together.

When a solid with tiny particles like sugar is placed in a liquid, occasionally a rapidly moving water molecule will ram against a sugar molecule, breaking its bond with the other sugar molecules. In time, all of the sugar molecules will become mixed with the water molecules. The process of solid molecules (but not atoms) breaking apart and mixing with the liquid molecules is called *dissolution*. The resulting liquid which is a combination of the original liquid plus the solid is called a *solution*. Stirring and heat both help the sugar to dissolve faster, since they both make the water molecules move faster, hastening the process.

Temperature and the Space Between Molecules

When molecules become hot, they move faster and they move away from each other, or *expand*. If the molecules in matter expand enough, they will change into another form, or state, of matter. When liquids become hot and expand, the molecules begin bouncing off each other, popping around. This is the movement you see when you see water boiling. When a gas becomes hot, its molecules also move very quickly and smash against each other, causing them to bounce off and spread out.

Just the Facts *(cont.)*

Temperature and the Space Between Molecules *(cont.)*

If the container which holds the gas is made of stretchy material, like the rubber in a balloon, the violent movement of the fast moving gas molecules will cause the material to spread out so the molecules can spread out. If the container is a hard material, the gas molecules will push harder against the walls. If there is a top on the container, it will likely pop off if a gas becomes very hot, due to the movement and expansion of the gas molecules.

When molecules are cold, they slow down and move closer together. This movement is called *contraction*. Contraction is easily seen in a balloon filled with air or gas. When the gas molecules become cold, they move closer together, deflating the balloon. If the molecules in matter contract enough, they change to another form, or state, of matter.

Expanding Molecules

Question

What will happen to cold molecules when they get warm?

Setting the Stage

- Tell students that molecules are always moving. The molecules in a solid can only vibrate against each other because they have strong bonds between them, but the molecules in liquids and gases can move more freely because their bonds are loose. In the next few days, the class will make some investigations about the movement of molecules, and what can affect the way molecules move.

- Show students a rubber band and pull it so that it stretches. Explain that action, going from a small form to a larger form, is called "expanding."

- Have teams act out being a solid molecule. Tell them that they are getting really hot. Ask them what they might do—would they want to stay huddled up, all hot and sticky?

- As they begin to move apart, tell them to "Freeze!" before they have completely formed a liquid. Point out that they have done just what the rubber band did—expanded, or changed from a small form to a larger form.

- Tell students that today they are going to do two short experiments in which they observe what happens to cold gas molecules as they get warm. They will have to observe carefully with their eyes and ears and brains.

- Show them any empty bottle. Ask them if any matter is in the bottle (elicit "gas"). Remind them that they should think about what was in the bottle when it was empty when they think about their hypothesis and conclusion.

- Tell them that in the first experiment they will have to work quickly and carefully. They will be working with cold bottles on which they will need to carefully place some water, then a quarter. They will then need to cover the bottle with their hands in order to warm it up. As they do this, they will have to be very careful not to knock the quarter off and they will have to be very quiet in order to make a good observation. Demonstrate to ensure understanding.

Materials Needed for Each Group

- one quarter
- a cold bottle (size of beer bottle)
- a balloon
- a cup with a little water
- Experiment Form (page 44)
- Observation Chart (page 45)

*Teacher Materials and Instructions: The bottles will need to be kept cold until the procedure step in which students use them. Let students make hypotheses, read procedures, before retrieving them. For the 2nd part of the experiment the teacher will also need a hot plate and a large, low pan with about 3 inches (7.5 cm) of water. The pan must accommodate the bottles from each team and the teams must be able to see the top of the bottles.

Expanding Molecules *(cont.)*

Procedure

1. Discuss the question. Thinking about what you have observed around you and learned in class, make a team hypothesis. Write it on your experiment sheet.

2. Follow the procedure steps on your experiment sheet. Be certain to check off each step as you do it. Be careful not to knock off the quarter and be quiet so you can use your ears in your observation.

3. Draw on the observation chart as events occur in the experiments.

4. Write the results of your experiment, telling what you actually saw happening. Talk about the materials you used in the experiment.

5. Discuss the conclusion. Remember that you are trying to answer the experiment question. Be sure that you have a because statement in the conclusion, and talk about the molecules.

Extensions

- To show that warm air will expand and some of the molecules will leave the space, make a balance scale with a small tuna can tied to one end and an empty plastic baby bottle tied upside down on the other end. Add rice or sand to the can if you need to balance it. Hold a lit candle under the open end of the bottle. As the air inside heats, some of the gas molecules will leave, the bottle will become lighter and the scale will tip.

- Have students write a story in which they pretend they are a gas molecule inside the bottle in their experiment today. They should write about what happened, including the space between themselves and the other molecules, and the introduction of heat.

Closure

- Discuss both observations and ask student Molecule teams to act out what they saw in each observation.

- Write an entry in the science journal—"Heat expands matter because it makes the molecules move faster and away from each other."

The Big Why

Students conduct two experiments in which they observe gas molecules expand when they get warm.

2387 Matter—Intermediate
How Do Molecules Act?

Expanding Molecules (cont.)

Science Experiment Form

Team Name_____ Date_____

Question (What do I want to find out?)

What will happen to cold gas molecules when they get warm?

Hypothesis (What do I think or guess will happen?)

_____

_____

Procedures (What are the steps to find out?)

Part 1

1. Get a cold bottle.
2. Put a little water on the top of the bottle and some on the quarter.
3. Put the quarter on top of the bottle, so that the opening is blocked.
4. Have everyone put their hands around the bottle so that the bottle gets warm. Be careful not to knock the quarter off the bottle.
5. Use your eyes and ears to observe what happens and record the results.

Part 2

1. Put a balloon over the top of your bottle. Be sure that the balloon covers the top of your bottle completely.
2. Give the bottle to your teacher to heat up.
3. Watch your bottle and balloon to see what happens and record the results.

Results (What did I see actually happen?)

1. Quarter on the bottle _____

2. Balloon on the bottle _____

Conclusion (What is the answer to the question?)

_____

_____

Expanding Molecules *(cont.)*

Observation Chart

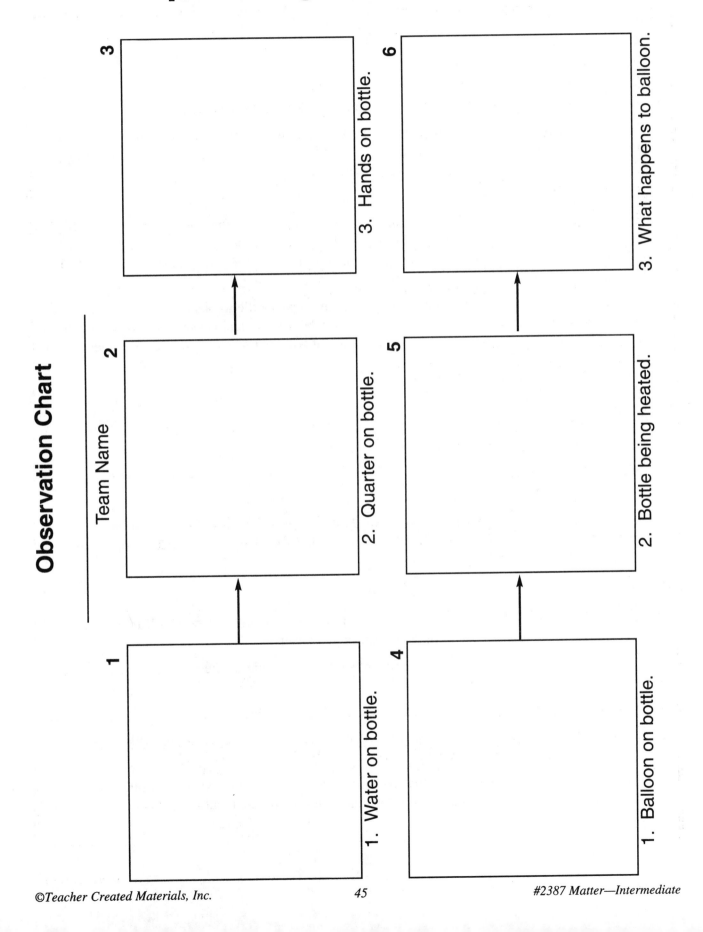

Team Name

1. Water on bottle.

2. Quarter on bottle.

3. Hands on bottle.

1. Balloon on bottle.

2. Bottle being heated.

3. What happens to balloon.

Contracting Molecules

Question

What will cold do to warm molecules?

Setting the Stage

- Review "expansion," and what warmth does to molecules and their movement.

- Show students a rubber band pulled taut, fully extended. Release the hand pressure so that the rubber band collapses. Tell students that this action is called "contraction." When something contracts, it moves from a larger form to a smaller form.

- Have students practice expanding and contracting their hands.

- Have a student team demonstrate molecules in a liquid. Tell them that they are getting really cold and they don't have any coats. What can they do? As they start to move closer, yell "Freeze" before they have assumed a solid molecule formation. Point out that they have "contracted," just like the rubber band.

- Tell students that today they will again work with an empty bottle to observe what happens to molecules when they get cold. Show them an empty bottle and again ask if there is any matter in it (elicit "gas"). Remind that they need to think about what is happening to the gas molecules in this experiment.

Materials Needed for Each Group

- one bottle (beer bottle size)

- a bowl with three ice cubes

- Experiment Form (page 48)

- Observation Chart (page 49)

*Teacher Materials: hot plate, large, low pan with about 3 inches (7.5 cm) of water. Pan must accommodate the bottles from each team and be low enough for students to observe the tops of the bottles.

Procedure

1. Discuss the question. Thinking about what you have observed around you and learned in class, make a team hypothesis. Write it on your experiment sheet.

2. Follow the procedure steps on your experiment sheet. Be certain to check off each step as you do it.

3. Draw the observation sequence as events occur in the experiment.

4. Write the results of your experiment, telling what you actually saw happening. Talk about the materials you used in the experiment.

5. Discuss the conclusion. Remember that you are trying to answer the experiment question. Be sure that you have a because statement in the conclusion, and talk about the molecules.

Contracting Molecules *(cont.)*

Extensions

- Try filling the little compartments of an ice cube tray with different liquids (e.g., honey, cooking oil, motor oil, water, vinegar, wine) making certain to label them. Place the ice cube tray in the freezer. Check it in an hour, two hours, the next day. Observe what happens to the liquids as they get cold.

- Have students write an explanation of how heat and cold affect matter for their parents.

Closure

- Discuss the observation and ask student molecule teams to act out what they saw in each observation.

- Write an entry in the science journal—"Cold contracts matter because it makes the molecules move closer together, then slow down."

The Big Why

Students conduct an experiment in which they observe gas molecules contracting when they get cold.

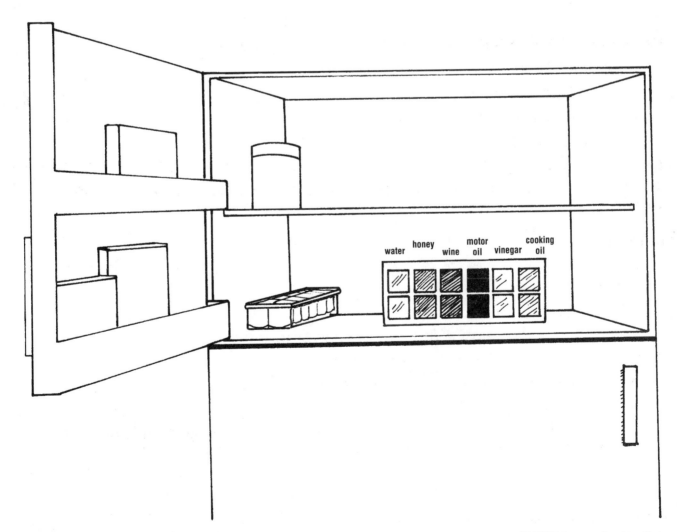

Contracting Molecules *(cont.)*

Science Experiment Form

Team Name_____ Date_____

Question (What do I want to find out?)
What will cold do to warm molecules?

Hypothesis (What do I think or guess will happen?)

_____

_____

Procedures (What are the steps to find out?)

1. Use your 1/4 cup measuring cup to put 3/4 cups of water into the bottle. Use your funnel.
2. Carefully put your balloon over the top of your bottle.
3. Take your bottle and balloon to the teacher to have it heated.
4. Feel the balloon to see if there is gas in it.
5. Put the bottle with the balloon on top in the bowl of ice cubes.
6. Use your eyes and hands to observe what happens to the balloon over the next 10 minutes.

Results (What did I see actually happen?)

_____

_____

_____

_____

Conclusion (What is the answer to the question?)

_____

_____

_____

Contracting Molecules *(cont.)*

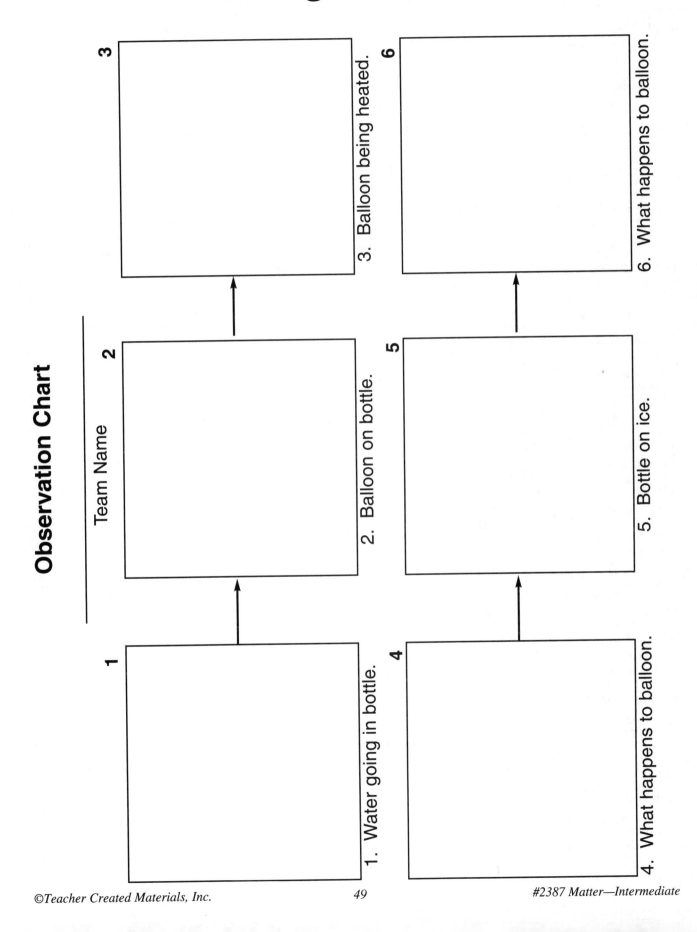

Observation Chart

Team Name

3.

2. Balloon on bottle.

3. Balloon being heated.

1. Water going in bottle.

4. What happens to balloon.

5. Bottle on ice.

6. What happens to balloon.

The Speed of Molecules

Question

Do hot or cold molecules move faster?

Setting the Stage

- Tell students that today they will be investigating the speed of hot and cold molecules. Pour a little food coloring into a glass of room temperature water. Have them observe the food coloring as the molecules move when they are neither very hot or very cold.

- Ask a team to come up to act like a liquid molecule team. Tell them to pretend that someone has heated up the floor under them and they are in their bare feet. As they start jumping, point out that they are moving faster because of the heat. They should also be moving further apart and expanding.

- Before letting the students begin the experiment, demonstrate that they must hold the food coloring bottles over the cups, but not squeeze them until the experiment reader/recorder, who will also be the counter, says "Ready, set, go!" Both food coloring handlers must be careful to just squeeze four drops into the cups after the "go" signal. They want to see if the heat or cold makes the food coloring spread faster, so the amount of food coloring must be the same, or the results might be affected.

Materials Needed for Each Group

- two clear plastic cups, one containing three ice cubes
- one container of water, a little more than 1 cup (250 mL)
- set of measuring cups
- two small bottles of food coloring
- Experiment Form (page 52)
- Observation Chart (page 53)

*Teacher Materials: hot plate, pan with warm water, ladle

Procedures

1. Discuss the question. Thinking about what you have observed around you and learned in class, make a team hypothesis. Write it on your experiment form.

2. Follow the procedure steps on your experiment form. Be certain to check off each step as you do it.

3. Draw on the observation chart as events occur in the experiment.

4. Write the results of your experiment, telling what you actually saw happening. Talk about the materials you used in the experiment.

5. Discuss the conclusion. Remember that you are trying to answer the experiment question. Be sure that you have a because statement in the conclusion, and talk about the molecules.

Extensions

- Try the same experiment in different liquids.
- Try the same experiment with varying temperatures of both hot and cold. Graph the results.

The Speed of Molecules *(cont.)*

Closure

- Discuss the observation and ask student molecule teams to act out what they saw in each observation.
- Write an entry in the science journal—"Warm molecules move faster than cold molecules."

The Big Why

Students conduct an experiment in which they observe the speed of cold and warm molecules.

The Speed of Molecules *(cont.)*

Science Experiment Form

Team Name_____   Date_____

Question (What do I want to find out?)
Do hot or cold molecules move faster?

Hypothesis (What do I think or guess will happen?)

_____

_____

Procedure (What are the steps to find out?)

1. Use your measuring cup to put 1/2 cup (125mL) of water in the plastic cup which has ice cubes in it.
2. Take the other cup, along with your 1/2 cup (125 mL) measuring cup, to the teacher to get 1/2 cup (125 mL) of warm water.
3. Open the bottles of food coloring and hold them over the cups of water.
4. When the counter says "Ready, set, go," squeeze both bottles of food coloring at exactly the same time. Squeeze the bottle four times, so four drops go into each cup.
5. Use your eyes to see what happens to the color of the water in each cup.

Results (What did I see actually happen?)

_____

_____

_____

Conclusion (What is the answer to the question?)

_____

_____

_____

The Speed of Molecules *(cont.)*

Observation Chart

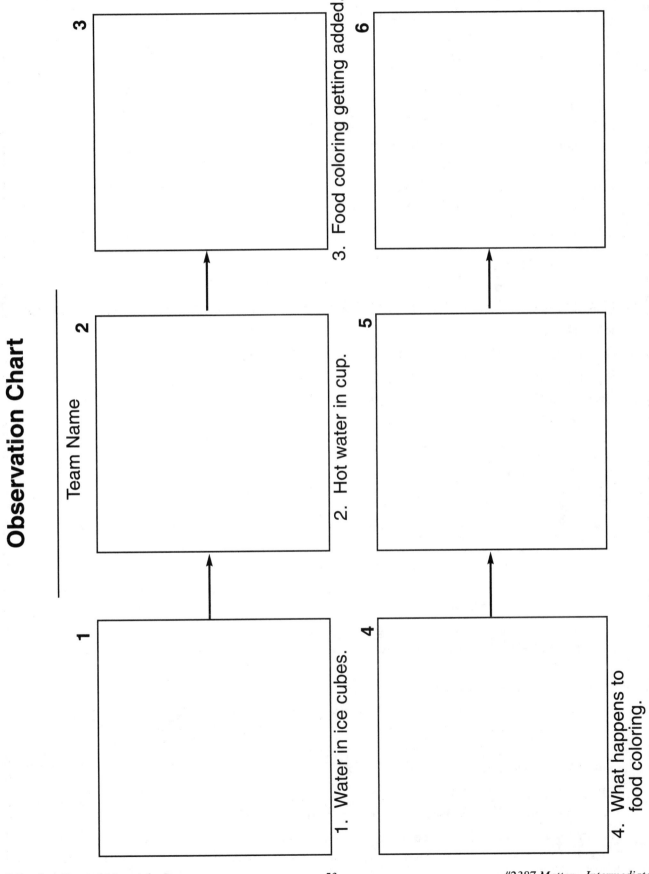

Team Name

1. Water in ice cubes.

2. Hot water in cup.

3. Food coloring getting added.

4. What happens to food coloring.

Dissolving Solids

Question

Will a solid dissolve faster in a hot or cold liquid?

Setting the Stage

- Review what happened in the experiment with hot and cold water. Have teams act out the three types of molecule teams with heat applied. They should both expand and move faster.
- Tell students that today they are going to learn about a new science term. When a solid is placed in a liquid and it falls apart, mixing with the liquid, it is said to "dissolve."
- They will conduct an experiment and observation in which they compare how fast a solid dissolves in hot and cold water. When they make their hypothesis, they need to think about what they have seen in their home and what they have learned in class about how molecules act.

Materials Needed for Each Group

- two clear plastic cups
- one ice cube in a bowl
- two sugar cubes
- two stirrers
- a cup containing a little more than 1 cup (250 mL) of water
- Experiment Form (page 56)
- Observation Chart (page 57)

*Teacher Materials: hot plate, pan with warm water, ladle

Procedure

1. Discuss the question. Thinking about what you have observed around you and learned in class, make a team hypothesis. Write it on your experiment form.
2. Follow the procedure steps on your experiment form. Be certain to check off each step as you do it.
3. Draw the observation chart as events occur in the experiment.
4. Write the results of your experiment, telling what you actually saw happening. Talk about the materials you used in the experiment.
5. Discuss the conclusion. Remember that you are trying to answer the experiment question. Be sure that you have a because statement in the conclusion, and talk about the molecules.

Extensions

- Keep a journal of solids in the home which are dissolved in liquids. Note whether the solid dissolves in a hot or cold liquid.
- Try putting a variety of loose solids in water to determine if they all will dissolve (e.g., salt, find sand, washing soda, baking soda, rice, jello).
- Time each to compare the dissolution rates.
- Try varying the heat of the water to see if the dissolution rates vary.
- Try stirring and not stirring to see if the dissolution rates vary.

54

Dissolving Solids *(cont.)*

Extensions *(cont.)*

- Measure the volume of the liquid before and after dissolving the solids. The volume will remain the same. Dissolved solids do not take up extra space.

Closure

- In the science journal, draw three boxes on a page. In the first box, draw a picture of a solid with its molecules. In the second box, draw a liquid being poured on a solid. Be sure to draw the liquid molecules. In the third box, draw a picture of the solid molecules collapsing and mixing up with the liquid. Label these pictures "dissolving."
- Write an entry in the science journal—"Solids dissolve faster in hot liquids."

The Big Why

Students conduct an experiment in which they compare the effect of heat and cold on the dissolution of matter.

Dissolving Solids *(cont.)*

Science Experiment Form

Team Name_____   Date_____

Question (What do I want to find out?)

Will a solid dissolve faster in hot water or cold water?

Hypothesis (What do I think or guess will happen?)

Procedures (What are the steps to find out?)

1. Put an ice cube in a clear plastic cup.
2. Use your measuring cup to put 3/4 cups (187.5 mL) of cold water in the cup with the ice.
3. Take your other clear plastic cup and your 1/4 cup (62.5 mL) measure to the teacher to get 3/4 cups (187.5 mL) of warm water.
4. Hold one sugar cube in each hand over the cups.
5. When the Counter says "Ready, set, go," drop the sugar cubes in the cups at the same time.
6. Use the stirrers to stir the water in each cup until the sugar cube dissolves.

Results (What did I see actually happen?)

_____

_____

_____

Conclusion (What is the answer to the question?)

_____

_____

_____

Dissolving Solids *(cont.)*

Observation Chart

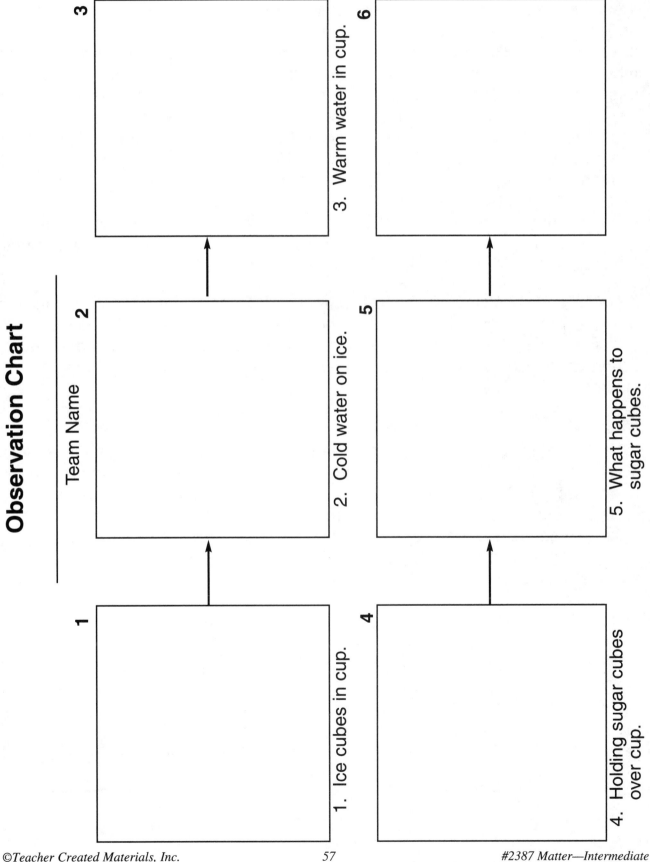

Team Name

1. Ice cubes in cup.

2. Cold water on ice.

3. Warm water in cup.

4. Holding sugar cubes over cup.

5. What happens to sugar cubes.

Just the Facts

The movement of molecules changes matter. When a solid, like ice, is heated, the molecules vibrate faster and move apart or expand. When it has vibrated enough, the bonds between the solid molecules loosen enough to move freely, or become a liquid. If even more heat is applied, the liquid molecules begin to move faster, loosening their bonds even more and bouncing harder and harder until they escape from the water in the form of a gas called water vapor. The changing of a liquid to a gas is called *evaporation*. Because molecules in a liquid have to break free to become a gas, the amount of liquid surface exposed to the air affects how fast it will evaporate. Hot water in a large bowl, for instance, will evaporate much faster than hot water in a bottle since the water molecules in the bottle only have the tiny space at the neck of the bottle to escape, while the molecules in the bowl have a large space from which they can escape. The rate of evaporation also increases as the temperature rises, since the molecules will move faster.

If matter becomes cold, the molecules move closer together or contract, and their movement slows down. If a gas becomes cold, its molecules slow down and its bonds tighten, turning into a liquid. The changing of a liquid to a gas is called *condensation*. When liquid molecules contract so much that they are close together, they have become a solid.

Chemical Change

When the atoms of a substance are rearranged, a chemical change takes place. The atoms of the different elements in the substance break apart and regroup themselves, forming a new substance. In water, for instance, a chemical change would take place if the water molecules were broken apart into hydrogen and oxygen molecules. Sometimes heat is required to make a chemical change, but sometimes the characteristics of the substances themselves can create the change.

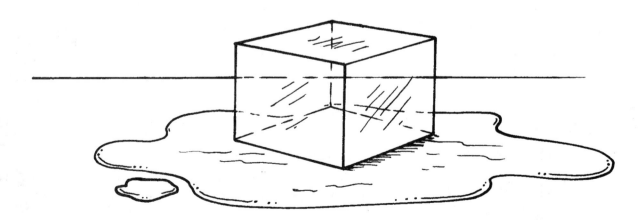

Hot Stuff

Question

Can heat change matter from one form to another?

Setting the Stage

- Have a student team come up and huddle like the molecules in a solid. Tell them to pretend that they are on the beach and it is very, very hot and they are all hot and sticky. As they move apart, ask the class what they are doing (expanding). When they have expanded to a liquid form yell "Freeze!" Ask the class what form of matter they have become now (a liquid). Point out that they have loosened their bonds.

- Ask the molecule team to pretend that they are on fire, getting hotter and hotter. Allow them to run away, breaking their bonds. Then yell "Freeze!" Point out that they have expanded so much that they really stretched their bonds and are now a gas.

- Hold up three ice cubes, ask students what kind of matter this is. Place the ice cubes into a pan and heat them. When the ice has melted, hold up the pan and ask them what kind of matter they see now. Keep heating the pan until all of the water has evaporated. Turn the pan upside down and ask the students where the water went (the water turned into a gas and escaped into the air in the room). Discuss what happened (the heat made the solid molecules keep expanding until they had become a gas).

Materials Needed for Each Group

- newspapers
- three bowls
- three heat sources (e.g., lamp, flashlight, hair dryer, etc.)
- three ice cubes
- data-capture sheet (page 61)

*Note: The teacher will need a pan, three ice cubes, and a hot plate for this demonstration.

Procedure

1. Record the time (to the minute) on your data-capture sheet.
2. Apply all of the heat sources to the ice cubes (e.g., turn on the lamp, flashlight, hair dryer). Be certain to hold all of them the same distance from the ice cube, in order to make a fair comparison about which heat source will change the matter fastest.
3. When all of your ice cubes have changed into a liquid, say "Time!," and the timer will tell you what time it is now. The data-capture sheet person must record the time and compute how many minutes have passed.
4. Complete the graph.

Extensions

- Have students look for examples of heat changing matter at home.
- Sit cups of water by the heater or in the sun. Have students mark the water line each day. Have them draw on the observation chart and draw conclusions about what happened to the water.

Hot Stuff *(cont.)*

Extensions *(cont.)*

- Have students write a story about the molecules in a snowman and what happens to them as the snowman sits all day in the sun.

Closure

- Discuss what happened to the solid molecules, emphasizing that in every case, it was heat which changed the matter. Have teams act out what happened.
- Make a science journal entry under "Principles of Matter"—"Heat can change matter from one form to another."

The Big Why

After acting out what happens to molecules when they get hot, students conduct an investigation in which they change the form of matter by applying various forms of heat.

Hot Stuff *(cont.)*

Team Name _____

Date _____

Heat Source	Time Heat Was Applied	Time Ice Melted	Time It Took Ice to Melt
Flashlight	_____	_____	_____ minutes
Lamp	_____	_____	_____ minutes
Hair Dryer	_____	_____	_____ minutes

1. Which heat source melted the ice first? _____

2. What observations have you made that explain why that heat source may have made the ice melt first? _____

3. Which heat source melted the ice last? _____

4. What observations have you made that explain why that heat source did not work as fast as the other two? _____

Cooling Off

Question

Can cold change matter from one form to another?

Setting the Stage

- Review the experiment in which students learned about cold contracting matter (the inflated balloon collapsed when put into ice water).

- Tell students that today they will be conducting an experiment in which cold is applied to different forms of matter.

- Have a team come to act like gas molecules. Tell them that is getting very, very cold and they are outside without coats. Ask the rest of the class to predict what they might do when they are getting so cold. Have the molecule team act out what they would do (get closer together to get warm). When they get close enough to join hands, ask the team to "Freeze." Ask the class what form of matter they have become (a liquid).

- Tell the molecule team that it is getting colder and colder, the wind is blowing, and it has started to snow—they still have no coats. What can they do? As they huddle together, ask what form of matter they have become (a solid).

- This experiment must be executed in two parts. The first part could take place the morning or day before the 2nd part.

Materials Needed for Each Team

- Experiment Form (page 64)
- Observation Chart (page 65)
- newspapers
- a clear cup
- one small bottle of food coloring
- 1/2 cup (125 mL) chipped ice
- a set of measuring cups
- a glass containing about a cup (250 mL) of water
- a stirrer

*Teacher Materials: one ice cube tray

*Note: The first part of this experiment must take place the afternoon or morning before the experiment.

Procedures

1. Discuss the question. Thinking about what you have observed around you and learned in class, make a team hypothesis. Write it on your experiment form.

2. Follow the procedure steps on your experiment form. Be certain to check off each step as you do them.

3. Draw on the observation chart as events occur in the experiment.

4. Write the results of your experiment, telling what you actually saw happening. Talk about the materials you used in the experiment.

Cooling Off (cont.)

Procedure (cont.)

5. Discuss the conclusion. Remember that you are trying to answer the experiment question. Be sure that you have a because statement in the conclusion, and talk about the molecules.

Extensions

- Place ice cubes in a pan, heat them until water vapor rises above the pan. Stand on a chair, holding a long stemmed wine glass upside down above the water vapor where the air is cool (use tongs to hold the stem of the glass). The cool air will condense the water vapor, turning it into water which will gather in the bowl of the glass. Allow the students to look at and feel the glass. Have them draw conclusions about how the water got in the glass.

- Have students use Venn diagrams to compare and contrast what heat and cold do to matter, then use the information in them to write an informative essay.

Closure

- Discuss student results and conclusions, having them act out the entire sequence of events, from the time the experiment began (when the water was put into the ice cube tray). Be certain that the students understand that the gas molecules in the room condensed or drew closer together as they hit the cold cup. They can be certain that the water on the outside is not from the inside of the cup, because that water is colored and the water on the outside is clear.

- Make a Science Journal entry under Principles of Matter: "Cold can change the form of matter."

The Big Why

After acting out what happens to molecules as they get cold, students conduct an experiment in which they see cold change the form of matter.

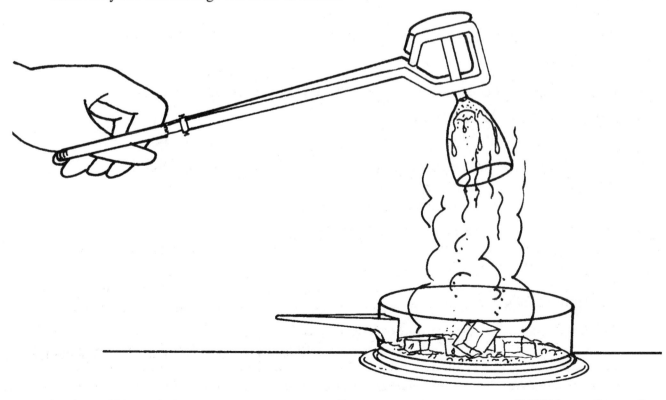

Cooling Off *(cont.)*

Science Experiment Form

Team Name_____   Date_____

Question (What do I want to find out?)
Can cold change matter from one form to another?

Hypothesis (What do I think or guess will happen?)

_____

_____

Procedures (What are the steps to find out?)
Part 1 (Morning or Afternoon before)
1. Pour some water into the ice cube tray.
2. Have your teacher put the ice cube tray in the freezer.
3. Complete Part 1 of your Observation Sequence. Label the boxes with the form of matter you saw and draw the molecules.

Part 2
1. Use your measuring cups to put 1/2 cup (125 mL) of water in your clear plastic cup.
2. Fill the rest of the cup with ice chips.
3. Squeeze four drops of food coloring into the cup.
4. Stir until the food coloring has spread and colored the water.
5. Let the cup sit for 10 minutes.
6. Examine the outside of the cup with your eyes and hands.
7. Complete your observation chart. Label the boxes with the form of matter you saw, and draw the molecules.

Results (What did I see actually happen?)
1. Water in the freezer _____

2. Air hitting cold cup _____

Conclusion (What is the answer to the question?)
_____

Cooling Off *(cont.)*

Observation Chart

Team Name

1. Water in tray.

→

2. Tray in freezer.

→

3. What happened to water.

4. Water and ice in cup.

→

5. Food coloring in cup.

→

6. What happens to cup.

It's a Gas!

Question

Can anything but heat and cold change the form of matter?

Setting the Stage

- Review the last two experiments, in which heat and cold changed the form of matter, having students act out what happened in the experiments as they portray molecule teams.
- Ask students to relate experiences and observations in their own lives in which they saw heat or cold change the form of matter.
- Ask them if they have ever seen anything but heat or cold change the form of matter.
- Tell them that the experiment which they will do today investigates that question. They must be very careful to follow the directions exactly.

Materials Needed for Each Group

- teaspoon measurers
- vinegar, a little over 1/4 cup (62.5 mL)
- a set of measuring cups
- a funnel
- baking soda, a little over 2 teaspoons (10 mL)
- one balloon
- Experiment Form (page 68)
- Observation Chart (page 69)

Procedure

1. Discuss the question. Thinking about what you have observed around you and learned in class, make a team hypothesis. Write it on your experiment form.
2. Follow the procedure steps on your experiment form. Be certain to check off each of the steps as you do them.
3. Draw on the observation form as events occur in the experiment.
4. Write the results of your experiment, telling what you actually saw happening. Talk about the materials you used in the experiment.
5. Discuss the conclusion. Remember that you are trying to answer the experiment question. Be sure that you have a because statement in the conclusion, and talk about the molecules.

Extensions

- Soak a ball of steel wool (a solid) with water (a liquid), and put it in a covered glass jar. Let it sit a few days until rust forms on the steel wool. The rust is a new form of matter (iron oxide), which was formed by a chemical reaction between water and the iron in steel.
- Get two cups. Put half a package of dry yeast into each cup, and pour 1/2 a cup (125 mL) of warm water over each cup. Add 1 teaspoon (5 mL) of sugar to one cup and watch what happens. It will bubble and an alcohol odor will be present. The chemical reaction between the yeast and the sugar has caused a breakdown into carbon dioxide and alcohol.

It's a Gas! *(cont.)*

Closure

- Review what the students observed in the experiment. The only things which were in the bottle were vinegar (a liquid) and baking soda (a solid). There was no heat or cold, yet they clearly saw a gas forming in the balloon. Tell them that what they saw was called a "chemical reaction." When certain kinds of matter get together, their molecular bonds are broken and the little pieces of the molecules which are called atoms break apart and make a different kind of matter.

- Make an entry in the Science Journal under Principles of Matter: "The molecules in two different kinds of matter can break apart to make a new kind of matter."

The Big Why

Students observe a chemical reaction changing the form of matter.

It's a Gas! *(cont.)*

Science Experiment Form

Team Name_____   Date_____

Question (What do I want to find out?)

Can anything but heat and cold change the state of matter?

Hypothesis (What do I think or guess will happen?)

_____

_____

Procedures (What are the steps to find out?)

1. With a funnel, put 2 teaspoons (10 mL) of baking soda into a balloon.
2. With a funnel, put 1/4 cup (62.5 mL) vinegar into the bottle.
3. Stretch the balloon top over the top of the bottle, being careful to let the "bag" part of the balloon hang over the side of the bottle.
4. Pick up the "bag" part of the balloon and let the baking soda go out of the balloon into the bottle.
5. Shake the bottle.
6. Observe with your eyes, ears, and hands to see what happens.

Results (What did I see actually happen?)

_____

_____

_____

Conclusion (What is the answer to the question?)

_____

_____

_____

It's a Gas! *(cont.)*

Observation Chart

Team Name

1. Baking soda in balloon.

2. Vinegar in bottle.

3. Balloon over top.

4. Baking soda goes in bottle.

5. Shake bottle.

6. What happens to balloon.

Just the Facts

A substance's density is the measure of weight of material within a certain volume. The weight is affected by how tightly packed the molecules are within that space. For instance, the molecules in a brick are very tightly packed, while the molecules in a block of wood the same size are more loosely packed. The brick contains more molecules, and thus weighs more. An object which has heavy weight for its size has a "high density," of tightly packed molecules, while an object which a has a light weight for its size has a "low density" of loosely packed molecules.

You can calculate the density of an object by dividing its weight by its volume. One cubic centimeter of water weighs one gram, so it has a density of one. If an object has a density greater than that of water (one), it will sink. If its density is less than one, it will float.

Floating and sinking are also affected by the shape of the object. The shape determines the amount of water the object will push out of the way or "displace." If the amount of water the object displaces is less than that of the amount of water, the object will float.

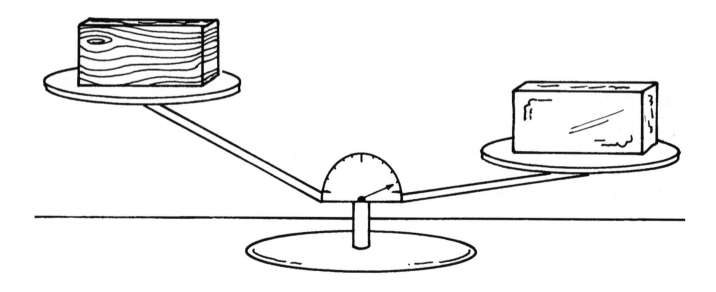

Introduction to Density

Question

What is density?

Setting the Stage

- Tell students that today they will learn about something called *density*. Ask them to recall the investigation they made about the weight of matter. In that investigation, they found that not all solids or liquids weigh the same. The reason they don't is because of the density of their molecules.

- When matter has molecules packed tightly into a specific space, we say that the matter has high density. When the molecules are not tightly packed into the same amount of space, we say that the matter has low density. The density of all three kinds of matter can be high or low.

- For the first part of their investigation today, the students will make models of high and low density matter. They will be pretending that beans are molecules. They will read the procedures, then glue the bean "molecules" on the square in the way the directions describe.

- In the second part of the investigation, they will make a hypothesis about whether the model that is most dense or the model that is least dense weighs more. Then they will test their hypothesis and put both models on a balance scale. (Demonstrate use of the balance scale, showing that a heavier object will push one side down.)

Materials Needed for Each Group

- about 1 1/2 cups of uncooked lima beans
- six file labels per team
- six-6" (15 cm) squares of construction paper (two blue, two green, two red)
- glue for every student
- a balance scale for teacher (or one per team, if available)
- data-capture sheet (page 73)

Procedure *(Student Instructions)*

1. Give the green squares to the gas model makers, the blue to the liquid model makers, and the red to the solid model makers.

2. For each type of matter, make two models. One model will have a high density of bean molecules, and one will have a low density of bean molecules. Here are some suggestions:

   Solid Models

   High Density: The beans should be tightly packed.
   Low Density: Just one end of the beans should be touching.

   Liquid Models

   High Density: The beans should be close together, but not touching.
   Low Density: The beans should be further apart, but not as far apart as a gas.

   Gas Models

   High Density: Put the beans just a little further apart than the low density liquid model.
   Low Density: Put the beans very, very far apart.

Introduction to Density *(cont.)*

Procedure *(cont.)*

3. After you are certain your beans are correctly placed, glue them to the paper.

4. Take a file label and write either "High density" or "Low density" on it to describe your model. Stick the label on your models.

5. Count how many bean molecules you have on each model and record them on your data-capture sheet.

6. Make a hypothesis about whether the high density or low density model of each type of matter will weigh more. Record your hypothesis on your data-capture sheet.

7. Take your models to the teacher to put on the balance scale to test your hypothesis about the weight. Record your results on your data-capture sheet.

8. Answer the rest of the questions on your data-capture sheet.

Extension

Have students closely examine different solids such as cork, wood, Styrofoam™, metal, etc., make hypotheses about their density. One way they might test density is by trying to poke a pencil through the object. They will be able to do so with low density objects, but not those with high density. Then have them weigh the objects to confirm the connection between density of molecules and weight.

Closure

- Compare team results, especially the "why" question on the data-capture sheet.

- Have students title a new page in their science journal "Density" and make an entry about what they learned today: "High density matter weighs more than low density matter."

The Big Why

Students make models of high and low density matter, then weigh them to determine the relationship between density and weight.

Introduction to Density *(cont.)*

Team Name _____

Date _____

Matter Model	Number of Beans	Weight Hypothesis	Weighing Results
Solid	High Density ___ Low Density ___	(Write "Light" or "Heavy") High Density ___ Low Density ___	(Write "Light" or "Heavy") High Density ___ Low Density ___
Liquid	High Density ___ Low Density ___	(Write "Light" or "Heavy") High Density ___ Low Density ___	(Write "Light" or "Heavy") High Density ___ Low Density ___
Gas	High Density ___ Low Density ___	(Write "Light" or "Heavy") High Density ___ Low Density ___	(Write "Light" or "Heavy") High Density ___ Low Density ___

In all three models, Gas, Liquid, Solid, which density weighed the most? _____

Look at the models and tell why you think they weighed the most. _____

Density of Liquids

Question

What will happen if different densities are poured together?

Setting the Stage

- Review the results of yesterday's investigation.

- Hold up a cork and a small heavy object, and have students come up to examine and hold them. Ask the class to make a hypothesis about what will happen if you place both of them in a jar of water. Put them in the water and allow students to test their hypotheses. Ask students why they think the heavy object sank, while the cork floated. They will probably say that the density of the heavy object was greater than that of the cork, but point out that another type of matter (water) was present. The heavy object had a greater density than that of the water, so it went lower, while the cork had a lower density than that of the water, so it stayed on top of the water.

- Today the class will investigate what happens when three types of liquids with varying densities are poured into the same place. They need to examine and feel their liquids before they make their hypotheses today, and they need to think about what they know about density when they make their hypotheses and draw conclusions.

Materials Needed for Each Group

- a large glass or jar
- a set of measuring cups
- one funnel
- in paper cups, a little over 1/2 cup (125 mL) of each: cooking oil, syrup, water
- a small bottle of food coloring (any color but yellow)
- Experiment Form (page 76)
- Observation Chart (page 77)

Procedure

1. Discuss the question. Thinking about what you have observed around you and learned in class, make a team hypothesis. Write it on your experiment form.

2. Follow the procedure steps on your experiment form. Be certain to check off each step as you do them.

3. Draw on the observation chart as events occur in the experiment.

4. Write the results of your experiment, telling what you actually saw happening. Talk about the materials you used in the experiment.

5. Discuss the conclusion. Remember that you are trying to answer the experiment question. Be sure that you have a because statement in the conclusion, and talk about the molecules.

Extensions

- Try adding alcohol to the water, after first measuring the amount of water and alcohol. Students will be astonished to see that the liquid amount actually will be a little less than the original amount of water. The alcohol molecules fit between the spaces of water molecules.

Density of Liquids *(cont.)*

Extensions *(cont.)*

- Pour some water and cooking oil in a jar, and screw the lid on tightly. Let students see that the oil has a lower density and floats on the water. Then shake the jar hard. When the jar sits again, the water and oil will return to their original positions—they cannot mix, due to the difference in their densities, no matter how hard you try to make it do so.

Closure

- Discuss the experiments, and ascertain how many hypotheses were confirmed. See if they related the weight of the liquids with their density.
- Make a science journal entry about what they learned today: "Liquids with lower densities will float on liquids with higher densities."

The Big Why

Students conduct an experiment in which they pour liquids together in order to ascertain that liquids of lower densities will float on liquids of higher densities.

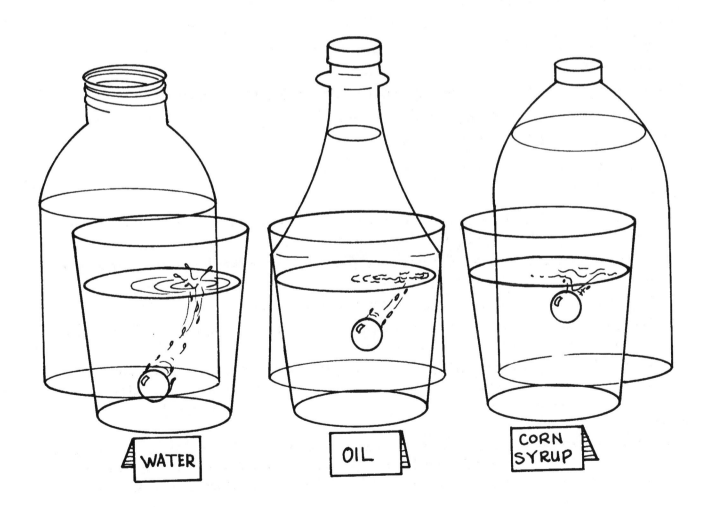

Density of Liquids *(cont.)*

Science Experiment Form

Team Name_____   Date_____

Question (What do I want to find out?)

What will happen if liquids of different densities are poured together?

Hypothesis (What do I think or guess will happen?)

_____

_____

Procedure (What are the steps to find out?)

1. Use your measuring cup to get 1/2 cup (125 mL) of syrup.
2. Pour the syrup in your glass, making sure to get all of it out.
3. Use your measuring cup to get 1/2 cup (125 mL) of cooking oil.
4. Use your funnel to carefully pour the oil along the side of the glass with the syrup in it.
5. Put six drops of food coloring into your cup of water. Let it sit until the water has colored.
6. Use your measuring cup to get 1/2 cup (125 mL) of water.
7. Use your funnel to carefully pour the water along the side of the glass with the syrup and oil.
8. Observe carefully.

Results (What did I see actually happen?)

_____

_____

Conclusion (What is the answer to the question?)

_____

_____

Density of Liquids *(cont.)*

Observation Chart

Team Name

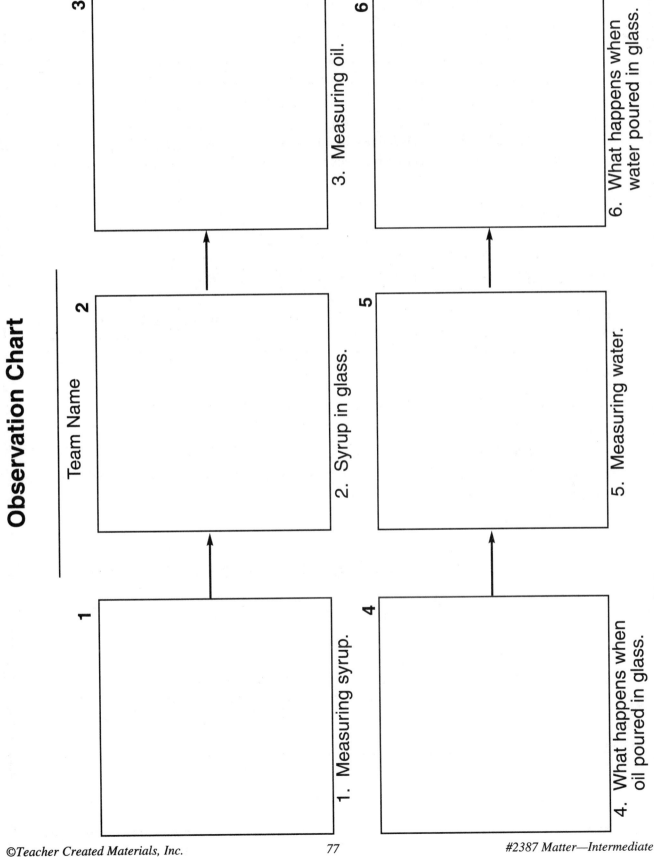

1. Measuring syrup.

2. Syrup in glass.

3. Measuring oil.

4. What happens when oil poured in glass.

5. Measuring water.

6. What happens when water poured in glass.

Floaters and Sinkers

Question
Can you guess which objects will sink and which will float?

Setting the Stage
- Review yesterday's experiment, discussing why the water floated on the syrup and why the oil floated on the water (the "floaters" had lower densities, so were lighter). Have students rank them from highest to lowest density.

- Tell students that today they will be comparing the density of solid objects with the density of water. Ask what will happen if an object with a density higher than water is dropped into the water (it will sink), or if an object with a density lower than water is dropped into the water (it will float).

- Hold up a piece of Styrofoam™ and piece of metal. Ask students if they have any idea how they might test these two objects to make a guess about the density of their molecules. Remind them that density indicates how closely packed their molecules are. Elicit something like "trying to poke a pencil into the object." If the object has a high density of molecules, the pencil point will not fit in the space between the object's molecules, but if the object has a low density of molecules, the pencil point will fit between the object's molecules. Demonstrate.

- Tell students that today they will be first testing solid objects to make a guess about their density. Then they will place the object in a glass of water to test whether the object's density is greater than or less than the density of water. As they work, their hypotheses should get better, since they will have comparisons to make.

Materials Needed for Each Group
- a large glass or jar
- a large number of small solid objects of varying density, but about the same size (e.g., cork, small piece of Styrofoam™, metal bar, rubber jacks ball, a piece of banana, a piece of candle, a piece of wood, a pin, a magnet, an eraser, a pair of scissors, etc.)
- data-capture sheet (page 80)

Procedure
1. Examine one of your solids. Feel it, try to poke a pencil through it to test its density.
2. Make a team hypothesis about whether the solid will float or sink in water. Remember that objects with a density greater than water sink. Objects with a density less than water float.
3. Place the solid in the water to test your hypothesis.
4. Record the results on your data-capture sheet.
5. Answer the question about the object's density on your data-capture sheet.
6. Repeat these steps with all the solids.

Extensions
- Try floating the same objects on different density liquids (e.g., syrup, oil, alcohol).

Floaters and Sinkers

Extensions *(cont.)*

- Further investigate floating and sinking by placing an empty, but stoppered medicine bottle into a pan of water. It will float because it is lighter than the same amount of water which would take up the same space. Fill half the bottle with water, stopper it, and place it in the pan again. It will sink, because the water plus the weight of the bottle make it heavier than the same amount of space the water would take up by itself.

Closure

- Discuss results, compare teams. Talk about whether their predictions got better as the investigation went on.

- Have students make a science journal entry about what they learned today: "Solids with a lower density than water will float, but solids with a density higher than water will sink."

The Big Why

Students conduct an investigation in which they test whether the density of solid objects are greater or less than that of water.

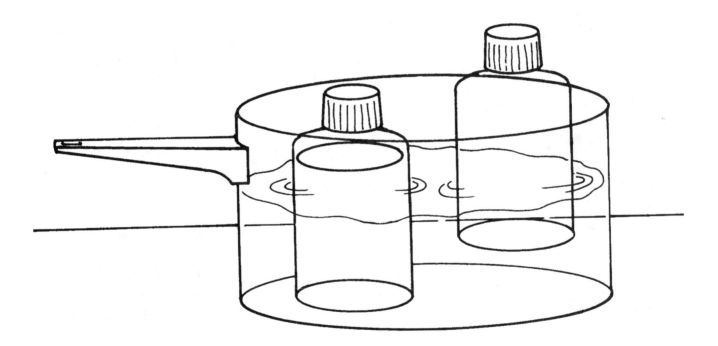

Floaters and Sinkers *(cont.)*

Team Name _____

Date _____

Solid	Hypothesis	Results	Density of Solid
	Float ____ Sink ____	Float ____ Sink ____	Density less than water ____ Density greater than water ____
	Float ____ Sink ____	Float ____ Sink ____	Density less than water ____ Density greater than water ____
	Float ____ Sink ____	Float ____ Sink ____	Density less than water ____ Density greater than water ____
	Float ____ Sink ____	Float ____ Sink ____	Density less than water ____ Density greater than water ____
	Float ____ Sink ____	Float ____ Sink ____	Density less than water ____ Density greater than water ____
	Float ____ Sink ____	Float ____ Sink ____	Density less than water ____ Density greater than water ____

Salt Water

Question
Can you change the density of water?

Setting the Stage
- Review the other experiments on density.
- Tell students that today they will be making an investigation about whether or not you can change the density of water. They will be putting a solid (salt) into some warm water, stirring it to dissolve. Ask how they can test if the density of water has changed. (First place an object which sinks in the water without salt, then put it in the water with salt, to see if the density has changed and it will now float.)
- Tell students that one of the solids they will be working with is an egg which has not been cooked. They will have to be very careful—if they break their egg, they will not be able to conduct their experiment. Show them how to use a spoon to carefully place the egg in water. They are not to just drop the egg into the glass, or it may crack.

Materials Needed for Each Group
- a large glass, half filled with warm water
- one set of measuring spoons
- a cup containing about 1/4 cup (62.5 mL) of salt
- one fresh egg
- a tablespoon (15 mL), from a table service, not a measuring spoon
- Experiment Form (page 83)
- Observation Chart (page 84)

Procedure
1. Discuss the question. Thinking about what you have observed around you and learned in class, make a team hypothesis. Write it on your experiment form.
2. Follow the procedure steps on your experiment form. Be certain to check off each step as you do them.
3. Draw on the observation chart as events occur in the experiment.
4. Write the results of your experiment, telling what you actually saw happening. Talk about the materials you used in the experiment.
5. Discuss the conclusion. Remember that you are trying to answer the experiment question. Be sure that you have a because statement in the conclusion, and talk about the molecules.

Extensions
- Fill a glass half full of warm water and again add three tablespoons (45 mL) of salt. Put a tablespoon on top of the water, slowly pour half a glass full of warm water which has no salt. The salt water should stay on the bottom, since it's density is greater. Carefully lower an egg into the glass with the tablespoon. It should sink below the fresh water, but float on the salt water. It will look as if it is suspended in the middle of the glass by magic.

Salt Water *(cont.)*

Extensions *(cont.)*

- Try floating some of the objects from the "Floaters and Sinkers" investigation to see if they float on salt water, even though they would not float on fresh water.

Closure

- Discuss why the egg sank in the fresh water (its density was greater than that of water), but floated on salt water (its density was less than that of salt water).
- Have students make an entry in their science journals about what they learned today: "Salt changes the density of water. Salt water has a higher density than fresh water."

The Big Why

Students conduct an experiment in which they see that the density of water can be changed.

Salt Water *(cont.)*

Science Experiment Form

Team Name_____ Date_____

Question (What do I want to find out?)

Can the density of water be changed?

Hypothesis (What do I think or guess will happen?)

_____

_____

Procedures (What are the steps to find out?)

1. Use your spoon to carefully and slowly lower your egg into your glass of fresh water.
2. Record what you see in the results section of this paper.
3. Take the egg out.
4. Use your tablespoon (tbls.) to carefully add 3 tablespoons (45 mL) of salt to the glass of fresh water.
5. Use the spoon to stir the water and salt until the salt crystals have all dissolved.
6. Use the spoon to carefully and slowly lower your egg into your glass of salt water.
7. Record what you see in the results section of this paper.

Results (What did I see actually happen?)

1. Egg in fresh water _____

2. Egg in salt water_____

Conclusion (What is the answer to the question?)

_____

_____

_____

Salt Water *(cont.)*

Observation Chart

Team Name

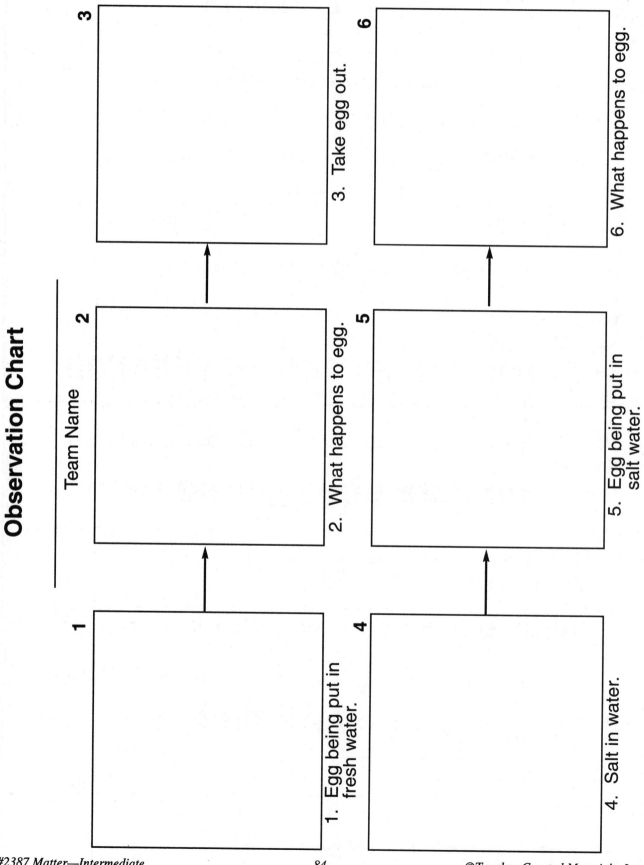

3

2

1
1. Egg being put in fresh water.

2. What happens to egg.

3. Take egg out.

6
6. What happens to egg.

5
5. Egg being put in salt water.

4
4. Salt in water.

Science Safety

Discuss the necessity for science safety rules. Reinforce the rules on this page or adapt them to meet the needs of your classroom. You may wish to reproduce the rules for each student or post them in the classroom.

1. Begin science activities only after all directions have been given.

2. Never put anything in your mouth unless it is required by the science experience.

3. Always wear safety goggles when participating in any lab experience.

4. Dispose of waste and recyclables in proper containers.

5. Follow classroom rules of behavior while participating in science experiences.

6. Review your basic class safety rules every time you conduct a science experience.

You can have fun and still be safe at the same time!

Matter Journal

Matter journals are an effective way to integrate science and language arts. Students are to record their observations, thoughts, and questions about past science experiences in a journal to be kept in the science area. The observations may be recorded in sentences or sketches which keep track of changes both in the science item or in the thoughts and discussions of the students.

Matter journal entries can be completed as a team effort or an individual activity. Be sure to model the making and recording of observations several times when introducing the journals to the science area.

Use the student recordings in the matter journals as a focus for class science discussions. You should lead these discussions and guide students with probing questions, but it is usually not necessary for you to give any explanation. Students come to accurate conclusions as a result of classmates' comments and your questioning. Matter journals can also become part of the students' portfolios and overall assessment program. Journals are valuable assessment tools for parent and student conferences as well.

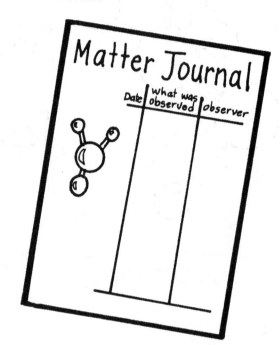

How to Make a Matter Journal

1. Cut two pieces of 8.5 " x 11" (22 cm x 28 cm) construction paper to create a cover. Reproduce page 87 and glue it to the front cover of the journal. Allow students to draw pictures of their experiments in the box on the cover.
2. Insert several matter journal pages. (See page 88.)
3. Staple the pages together and cover the stapled edge with book tape.

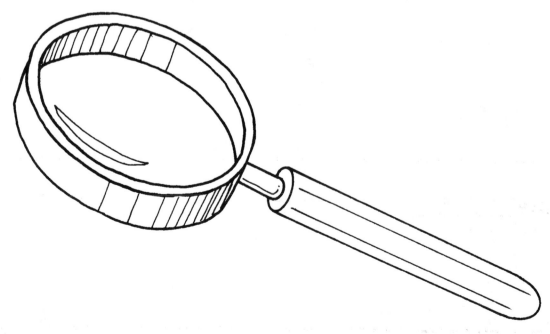

My Matter Journal

Name _____

Matter Journal

Illustration

This is what happened: _____

_____

_____

_____

_____

This is what I learned: _____

_____

_____

_____

_____

My Science Activity

K-W-L Strategy

Answer each question about the topic you have chosen.

Topic: _____

K—What I already **know:** _____

_____

_____

_____

_____

W—What I **want to find out:** _____

_____

_____

_____

_____

L—What I **learned after doing the activity:** _____

_____

_____

_____

_____

Investigation Planner *(Option 1)*

Observation

_____

_____

Question

_____

_____

Hypothesis

_____

_____

Procedure

  Materials Needed:

_____

_____

_____

_____

  Step-by-Step Directions: (Number each step.)

_____

_____

_____

_____

_____

_____

Investigation Planner *(Option 2)*

Science Experience Form

Scientist _____

Title of Activity _____

Observation: What caused us to ask the question?

_____

_____

_____

Question: What do we want to find out?

_____

_____

_____

Hypothesis: What do we think we will find out?

_____

_____

_____

Procedure: How will we find out? (List step by step.)

_____

_____

_____

_____

Results: What actually happened?

_____

_____

_____

Conclusions: What did we learn?

_____

_____

Assessment Forms

The following chart can be used by the teacher to rate cooperative learning groups in a variety of settings.

Science Groups Evaluation Sheet

Room: _____ Date: _____

Activity: _____

Everyone

. . . gets started.

. . . participates.

. . . knows jobs.

. . . solves group problems.

. . . cooperates.

. . . keeps noise down.

. . . encourages others.

Group									
1	2	3	4	5	6	7	8	9	10

Teacher Comment

_____

Bragging rights for the group session: _____

_____

Assessment Forms *(cont.)*

The evaluation form below provides student groups with the opportunity to evaluate the group's overall success.

Cooperative Group Evaluation

Assignment: _____

Date: _____

Scientists   Jobs

_____   _____

_____   _____

_____   _____

_____   _____

As a group, decide which face you should fill in and complete the remaining sentences.

1. We finished our assignment on time, and we did a good job.
2. We encouraged each other, and we cooperated with each other.

3. We did best at _____

_____

4. Next time we could improve at_____

_____

Super Scientist Award

This is to certify that

_____
Name

made a science discovery.

Congratulations!

_____
Teacher

_____
Date

Super Scientist

Glossary

Atom—The smallest particle of matter that can exist. Molecules are made up of tiny atoms.

Chemical Reaction—The breaking apart of the atoms within a molecule. The atoms rearrange themselves into separate substances.

Conclusion—The outcome of an investigation.

Condensation—The process of a gas cooling and becoming a liquid.

Contract—To grow smaller or get smaller in size. Molecules contract when cooled.

Density—The heaviness of a substance. The measurement of the mass of a specific volume.

Diffusion—The movement of molecules from one place to another resulting in a even distribution of molecules.

Displacement—The amount of water an object can push away.

Dissolve—The breaking down and mixing of a solid's molecules with those of a liquid.

Evaporation—The process of a liquid or solid being heated and becoming a gas, or vapor.

Expand—To grow larger, take up more space. Molecules expand when heated.

Experiment—A means of proving or disproving an hypothesis.

Gas—A form of matter which has no definite shape or volume. The molecules are widely spaced.

Hypothesis—An educated guess to a question which you are trying to answer.

Investigation—Observation of something followed by a systematic inquiry in order to explain what was originally observed.

Liquid—A form of matter which has definite volume, but no definite shape. There is space between the molecules.

Mass—Volume

Matter—Anything that has weight and takes up space.

Molecule—A group of atoms; the smallest part of a substance which can exist and still retain the characteristics of the substance.

Observation—Careful notice or examination of something.

Procedure—The series of steps carried out in an experiment.

Results—The data collected after an experiment.

Scientific Method—A creative and systematic process of proving or disproving a given question, following an observation. It includes observation, question, hypothesis, procedure, results, conclusion, and future investigations.

Scientific Process Skills—The skills necessary to be able to think critically. Process skills include observing, communicating, comparing, ordering, categorizing, relating, inferring, and applying.

Solid—A form of matter which has definite volume and shape. The molecules are close together.

Solution—A uniform mixture of dissolved solids.

Volume—The amount of space something takes up. Mathematically it is determined by multiplying together an item's width, length, and height.

Water Vapor—The "gas" state of water.

Bibliography

Ardley, Neil. *Hot & Cold.* Gulliver Books, 1992.

Ardley, Neil. *The Science of Air.* Gulliver Books, 1991.

Ardley, Neil. *Working with Water.* Franklin Watts, 1983.

Arnov, Boris. *Water: Experiments to Understand It.* Lothrop, Lee & Shepard Books, 1980.

Challand, Helen J. *Activities in the Physical Sciences.* Childrens Press, 1984.

Chisholm, Jane & Mary Johnson. *Introduction to Chemistry*. Usborn Publishing Ltd., 1983.

Cooper, Christopher. *Matter.* Dorling Kindersley, Inc., 1992.

Darling, David. *Between Heat and Cold: The Science of Heat.* Dillon Press, 1992.

Henbest, Nigel & Heather Couper. *Physics.* Franklin Watts, 1983.

Hillen, Judith, Evalyn Hoover & Sheryl Mercier (Eds.). *Primarily Physics. Project AIMS.* AIMS Education Foundation, 1990.

Hieeln, Judith, Arthur Wiebe & Dave Youngs (Eds.). *Water, Precious Water. Project AIMS.* AIMS Education Foundation, 1988.

Kilburn, Robert E. & Pater S. Howell. *Exploring Physical Science.* Allyn & Bacon, 1981.

Levenson, Elaine. *Teaching Children about Science.* Prentice Hall Press, 1985.

Lorbeer, George C. *Science Activities for Young Children.* Volume Two. Wm. C. Brown, 1993.

Lorbeer, George C. *Science Activities for Young Children.* Volume One. Wm. C. Brown, 1992.

Mandell, Muriel. *Simple Science Experiment with Everyday Materials.* Sterling, 1990.

Mandell, Muriel. *Physics Experiments for Children.* Dover Publications, 1968.

Mebane, Robert C. & Thomas R. Rybolt. *Adventures with Atoms and Molecules.* Enslow, 1985.

The New Book of Popular Science. Volume 3, Physical Sciences, General Biology, 1990, Grolier

VanCleave, Janice. *Molecules.* John Wiley & Sons, Inc., 1993.

VanCleave, Janice. *Chemistry for Every Kid.* John Wiley & Sons, Inc., 1989.

Walpole, Brenda. *Water.* Warwick Press, 1987.

Ward, Alan. *Water and Floating.* Franklin Watts, 1992.

Watson, Philip. *Liquid Magic.* Lothrop, Lee & Shephard Books, 1982.

Wellnitz, William R. *Be a Kid Physicist.* Tab Books, 1993.

White, Nancy. *Air and Water. Macmillan Early Science Activities.* Newbridge Communications, Inc., 1991.

Wiebe, Arthur, Larry Ecklund & Judith Hillen (Eds.) *Seasoning Math and Science, Spring & Summer, Second Grade.* Project AIMS. AIMS Education Foundation, 1987.

Wilkin, Fred. *Matter. A New True Book.* Childrens Press, 1986.

Wingate, Philippa. *Essential Physics.* Usborne Publishing, Ltd., 1991.

Wood, Robert W. *Science for Kids.* Tab Books, 1991.

Worosz, Michael. *States of Matter. A Delta Science Module.* Delta Education, Inc., 1988.